THE SEVEN CHURCHES OF ASIA AND THEIR WORKS

Prophetic Messages and Their Relevance to Today's Churches

Dr. Maxwell Shimba

Printed by Shimba Publishing LLC
Printed in the United States of America

TABLE OF CONTENTS

INTRODUCTION

The Book of Revelation, often called the Apocalypse, contains many profound mysteries and prophetic messages. One of its most striking and practical sections is the letters to the seven churches of Asia, found in chapters 2 and 3. Written by the apostle John under the direct revelation of Jesus Christ, these letters were addressed to specific congregations in the Roman province of Asia (modern-day Turkey). Each church received a personalized message from the risen Christ, containing praise, rebuke, encouragement, or warning.

The seven churches—Ephesus, Smyrna, Pergamum, Thyatira, Sardis, Philadelphia, and Laodicea—were real historical communities facing unique challenges in their faith and spiritual life. However, the messages they received have transcended time and geography, providing insight for churches throughout history. Their condition represents not only their own spiritual states but also types of churches and believers that exist in every generation. Through their example, we gain valuable lessons on what pleases the Lord and what displeases Him.

What stands out in these letters is Jesus' emphasis on works. While faith is the foundation of the Christian life, the letters to the seven churches show that faith must be demonstrated through works. The churches are commended or rebuked based on their actions—how they lived out their faith. Jesus repeatedly says, "I know your works," signaling that He closely observes how believers live. The letters show that works of love, obedience, perseverance, and service are critical in maintaining a vibrant relationship with God. At the same time, these letters warn against spiritual complacency, compromise, and sin, which can damage that relationship.

In today's context, many churches struggle with the same issues that the seven churches faced. Some have lost their first love, growing cold and mechanical in their worship. Others face persecution and are called to remain faithful despite suffering. Still others are tempted to compromise with the world or tolerate false teachings. Jesus' warnings against lukewarmness and spiritual death are especially relevant in an age where material comfort can lead to spiritual apathy.

As we journey through the messages to each of the seven churches, we will explore the following themes:

- Faith and Works: How the balance between faith and works is central to a healthy Christian life and how Jesus evaluates the works of His people.

- Spiritual Vigilance: The need for churches to remain watchful and alert, avoiding complacency and compromise.

- Endurance in Persecution: The call to persevere through trials and suffering, with the promise of eternal rewards for those who remain faithful.

- Repentance and Renewal: The recurring theme of repentance as a means of restoring and renewing one's relationship with Christ.

This book not only explores the historical and theological context of each church but also draws parallels between their spiritual condition and the challenges that modern churches face. The prophetic messages are as relevant today as they were in the first century, calling every believer to examine their works, their faith, and their devotion to Christ.

As you read through the letters, consider this: If Jesus were to write a letter to your church or your own spiritual life, what would He say? Would He commend you for your love, faithfulness, and perseverance, or would He call you to repent and return to Him? This is the ultimate question that these letters present.

The churches of Asia teach us that salvation is not based on works, but works are the fruit of a living faith. Without them, faith becomes barren and lifeless. Jesus is looking for overcomers—those who will endure in faith and demonstrate their love through obedience until the end. The promise to the overcomer is great: eternal life, power over the nations, a new name, and a place in God's kingdom. As we delve into these profound messages, may we find inspiration to strengthen our faith and works and walk more closely with our Lord.

Let us begin the journey by exploring the first of the seven churches: Ephesus, the church that had lost its first love.

DR. MAXWELL SHIMBA

CHAPTER 01

EPHESUS – THE CHURCH THAT LOST ITS FIRST LOVE

Scripture Reference: Revelation 2:1-7

"Unto the angel of the church of Ephesus write; These things saith he that holdeth the seven stars in his right hand, who walketh in the midst of the seven golden candlesticks; I know thy works, and thy labour, and thy patience, and how thou canst not bear them which are evil: and thou hast tried them which say they are apostles, and are not, and hast found them liars: And hast borne, and hast patience, and for my name's sake hast laboured, and hast not fainted. Nevertheless, I have somewhat against thee, because thou hast left thy first love. Remember therefore from whence thou art fallen, and repent, and do the first works; or else I will come unto thee quickly, and will remove thy candlestick out of his place, except thou repent. But this thou hast, that thou hatest the deeds of the Nicolaitanes, which I also hate. He that hath an ear, let him hear what the Spirit saith unto the churches; To him that overcometh will I give to eat of the tree of life, which is in the midst of the paradise of God."

Introduction to Ephesus

The city of Ephesus was one of the most important cities in Asia Minor during the Roman Empire, both commercially and spiritually. It was a hub of pagan worship, particularly devoted to the goddess Artemis (Diana of the Ephesians) (Acts 19:27), but it was also a center for early Christian evangelism, with the Apostle Paul spending considerable time there during his missionary journeys (Acts 18:19; 19:1-10). Ephesus was known for its dedication to the teachings of Christ and its rigorous defense of doctrinal purity.

The church in Ephesus had a history of being a beacon of faithfulness, receiving notable teaching from apostles such as Paul, John, and Timothy. However, in this letter, we see that despite their outward success in works, they had lost something very vital: their first love.

Christ's Introduction: The One Who Holds the Seven Stars (Rev. 2:1)

The letter to the church in Ephesus begins with a powerful description of Jesus: He is the one who "holds the seven stars in His right hand" and "walks in the midst of the seven golden lampstands." The seven stars (Greek: "ἄστρα," aster, Strong's G792) represent the messengers or leaders of the seven churches (Rev. 1:20), while the lampstands (Greek: "λυχνία," lychnia, Strong's G3087) symbolize the churches themselves.

This description reminds the Ephesian church that Christ is in complete control and authority over His church. He holds the leadership in His right hand, the hand of power, and walks among the churches, symbolizing His intimate presence and watchfulness. No detail escapes His sight. He knows every work, every strength, and every weakness of His people.

Commendation: Works, Labor, Patience (Rev. 2:2-3)

Jesus begins by acknowledging the strengths of the Ephesian church:

- "I know thy works": The term "works" (Greek: "ἔργα," erga, Strong's G2041) emphasizes their deeds and actions. The church at Ephesus was not idle; they were actively engaged in service for the Kingdom of God. Their works reflected a church deeply involved in ministry and service.

- "Thy labour": The word "labour" (Greek: "κόπος," kopos, Strong's G2873) refers to toil that results in weariness. The Ephesian church was diligent in their efforts to spread the Gospel and protect the truth, even to the point of exhaustion.

- "Patience": The Greek word "ὑπομονή" (hypomonē, Strong's G5281) is often translated as "endurance" or "steadfastness." The Ephesians were able to patiently endure hardship and persevere under pressure. They had faced opposition, trials, and challenges, yet remained firm in their faith.

- "Thou canst not bear them which are evil": This phrase highlights the Ephesian church's refusal to tolerate sin or falsehood. They tested those who claimed to be apostles but were not, identifying them as liars. The church had discernment and was committed to doctrinal purity (1 John 4:1).

The Problem: "Thou Hast Left Thy First Love" (Rev. 2:4)

Despite these positive attributes, Jesus offers a sharp rebuke: "Nevertheless, I have somewhat against thee, because thou hast left thy first love." The word "left" (Greek: "ἀφίημι," aphiēmi, Strong's G863) suggests abandonment or neglect. The Ephesian believers had not outright rejected Christ, but their fervor and passion for Him had diminished.

- What is the "first love"? The "first love" refers to the early, passionate devotion the church once had for Christ. When they first believed, their love for Him overflowed into their works and ministry. Over time, however, their service had become more mechanical, dutiful, and perhaps even legalistic. They were still active in ministry, but the motivation behind their works had shifted. Love had taken a backseat to duty.

Jesus emphasizes the importance of love in the Christian walk. Love is the foundation of all Christian works (Matthew 22:37-40; 1 Corinthians 13:1-3). Without love, even the most impressive works are empty. The church in Ephesus had grown cold in their affection for Christ, and that spiritual coldness was a serious issue in the eyes of the Lord.

The Call to Repent: Remember, Repent, and Return (Rev. 2:5)

Jesus gives the Ephesians a three-step process to restore their relationship with Him:

1. Remember: "Remember therefore from whence thou art fallen." The first step in returning to their first love was to remember where they had been spiritually. The Greek word "μνημόνευε" (mnēmoneuō, Strong's G3421) means to recall or keep in mind. Jesus calls them to reflect on their former devotion and realize how far they had fallen.

2. Repent: The next step is repentance. The Greek word "μετανοέω" (metanoeō, Strong's G3340) means a change of mind that results in a change of behavior.

Repentance is not just feeling sorry for drifting away; it involves a deliberate turning back to God, realigning their hearts with their original devotion.

3. Do the first works: Jesus calls them to return to the "first works"—the deeds motivated by love, not merely duty or habit. The works themselves were important, but the motivation behind them was critical. A return to those early expressions of love and faithfulness would restore the vitality of their relationship with Christ.

The Warning: Removal of the Candlestick (Rev. 2:5)

Jesus issues a stern warning to the church: "I will come unto thee quickly, and will remove thy candlestick out of his place, except thou repent." The removal of the candlestick symbolizes the removal of the church's influence or even its existence. A church that loses its love for Christ and continues to neglect that love is at risk of spiritual death. Without the light of love, the church's witness dims, and its influence in the world is lost.

This warning highlights the seriousness of spiritual coldness. It is not enough to maintain doctrinal purity or be active in ministry; the church must be fueled by a love for Christ. The absence of love threatens the very life of the church.

Encouragement: Hatred of the Nicolaitanes (Rev. 2:6)

Despite the rebuke, Jesus offers a word of commendation: "But this thou hast, that thou hatest the deeds of the Nicolaitanes, which I also hate." The Nicolaitanes were a sect known for promoting a lifestyle of compromise and indulgence, possibly advocating that believers could participate in pagan practices without harm. The Ephesian church rightly rejected this heresy.

The Promise to the Overcomer (Rev. 2:7)

The letter closes with a promise: "To him that overcometh will I give to eat of the tree of life, which is in the midst of the paradise of God." The tree of life (Greek: "ξύλον ζωῆς," xylon zōēs, Strong's G3586 and G2222) symbolizes eternal life, a return to the state of perfection lost in Eden. The "overcomer" (Greek: "νικῶν," nikōn, Strong's G3528) is the one who, through faith and perseverance, remains faithful to Christ and does not lose his love for Him.

The promise of eternal life in the paradise (Greek: "παράδεισος," paradeisos, Strong's G3857) of God is a beautiful reminder of the ultimate reward for those who endure in love and faithfulness to Christ.

The Warning: Removal of the Candlestick (Rev. 2:5)

Jesus issues a sobering warning: "I will come unto thee quickly, and will remove thy candlestick out of his place, except thou repent." This statement underscores the gravity of their spiritual condition. The candlestick (Greek: "λυχνία," lychnia, Strong's G3087) represents the church itself, its light, and its witness. For the Ephesian church, the removal of their candlestick would mean the loss of their position and influence as a true church of Christ.

This is a stark reminder that no amount of good works or doctrinal purity can compensate for a lack of love. A church without love cannot effectively represent Christ, the Light of the World (John 8:12). Their spiritual vibrancy was at risk, and unless they repented, Jesus would intervene by removing their influence, rendering them ineffective in their mission.

A Commendation: Hating the Deeds of the Nicolaitans (Rev. 2:6)

Despite the strong rebuke, Jesus commends the Ephesians for hating the deeds of the Nicolaitans (Greek: "Νικολαΐτης," Nikolaitēs, Strong's G3531), which He also hates. Although little is known about this group, it is generally believed that they promoted a form of licentiousness, distorting Christian liberty into moral permissiveness. Jesus acknowledges that the Ephesians maintained a strong stance against these corrupt practices, further affirming their commitment to doctrinal purity.

The Promise to the Overcomer (Rev. 2:7)

The letter concludes with a promise to those who overcome: "To him that overcometh will I give to eat of the tree of life, which is in the midst of the paradise of God."

The term "overcome" (Greek: "νικάω," nikaō, Strong's G3528) is a recurring theme in Revelation, referring to those who remain faithful in the face of trials and spiritual challenges. The reward for the overcomer is access to the tree of life (Greek: "ξύλον ζωῆς," xylon zōēs, Strong's G3586 and G2222), a direct reference to the tree in the Garden of Eden (Genesis 2:9; 3:22) and symbolic of eternal life and communion with God. This tree, located in the paradise of God (Greek: "παράδεισος," paradeisos, Strong's G3857), represents the restoration of humanity's access to eternal life, which was lost due to sin but restored through Christ (Revelation 22:2).

The Call to Renew First Love

The letter to the church of Ephesus is a powerful reminder that faithfulness to Christ involves both works and love. While the Ephesians excelled in doctrinal purity, discernment, and labor, they had allowed their love for Christ to grow cold. Jesus calls them—and all believers today—to return to their "first love," to rekindle that initial fervor and passion that characterized their early walk with Him.

The message to Ephesus serves as a warning to all churches and individual believers: it is possible to be busy with religious activities and still drift away from the core of what it means to follow Christ. Love must be at the heart of everything we do, for without it, our works are hollow. Jesus desires a church that not only guards truth but also passionately loves Him, reflecting His love in the world.

For those who heed this call and return to their first love, the promise is profound: they will overcome and partake of eternal life in the presence of God, restored to the fullness of His paradise.

May we, like the Ephesian church, remember where we have fallen, repent, and return to the love that first ignited our hearts for Christ. Only then can we truly fulfill our purpose and experience the fullness of life that God promises to those who love Him.

Application for Today—The Call to Rekindle First Love

The message to the church of Ephesus carries profound significance for today's churches. Like the Ephesians, many churches in the modern era are diligent in doctrinal precision and committed to service, yet they may gradually lose their spiritual fervor. The warning to Ephesus is not just a historical account but a living message to all believers who face the same dangers of losing the passion and love that first drew them to Christ.

Diligence Without Devotion

The Ephesian church was commended for its hard work, patience, and intolerance of evil, which echoes many congregations today. Churches are often full of good works—community outreach, charity, Bible study, and sound doctrine. However, in the midst of busyness, there is the danger of neglecting the most important element: a deep, passionate relationship with Christ. As with Ephesus, doctrinal soundness without the foundation of love can lead to a mechanical faith, one that focuses more on service than on sincere devotion to God.

Paul, writing to the Corinthians, reminds us that without love, even the most impressive works or knowledge amounts to nothing (1 Corinthians 13:1-3). Churches and believers can become like "sounding brass"—making noise without genuine spiritual substance. The first and greatest commandment, according to Jesus, is to love the Lord with all our heart, soul, and mind (Matthew 22:37). This heartfelt love should be the motivation behind all service and ministry.

The Call to Repent and Return

Jesus' admonition to Ephesus to "repent and do the first works" (Revelation 2:5) is a call to every believer and congregation that has drifted from its passionate relationship with Christ. The "first works" signify those actions that spring from a heart of love and devotion, the joy and zeal that characterized the early days of walking with Christ. Jesus does not simply ask for more works but for a return to the proper motivation behind those works—love for Him.

This is a crucial reminder that revival and spiritual renewal are not found in merely increasing church activities or programs. Instead, they are found in rekindling a deep, personal relationship with Christ. Churches today are called to introspectively ask: Have we lost our first love? Have we become too focused on tradition, organization, or even good works while neglecting the vibrancy of our relationship with Jesus?

Warning and Promise

The warning to Ephesus—that their candlestick would be removed unless they repented—applies just as much today as it did in the first century. A church that loses its love for Christ and fails to respond to His call for repentance risks losing its effectiveness and witness. Churches that are more concerned with maintaining religious practices than with cultivating a passionate love for Jesus may find themselves spiritually lifeless, despite all outward appearances.

But with the warning comes the promise: for those who overcome and rekindle their love for Christ, there is the assurance of eternal life—symbolized by the tree of life in the paradise of God (Revelation 2:7). This promise invites believers to hold on to their faith, restore their devotion, and persevere, knowing that the reward is everlasting communion with God.

Personal Application: Rekindling Our Love

This message applies not only to churches but also to individual believers. Every Christian is called to examine their personal relationship with Christ. Has the fire that once burned brightly become a flicker? Has the routine of Christian life replaced a deep love for Jesus? The warning to Ephesus is a personal invitation to each believer to return to the simplicity and passion of their initial relationship with Christ.

Practical steps for rekindling our first love may include:

- Personal Devotion: Spending intentional time in prayer, worship, and Scripture study—not out of obligation, but out of a genuine desire to grow closer to Christ.

- Reflection and Repentance: Asking the Holy Spirit to reveal any areas where love has grown cold, and repenting for putting works or other priorities ahead of love for Christ.

- Action Based on Love: Renewing commitment to serve, not out of routine, but motivated by love for Jesus and for others.

The Need for Spiritual Renewal in Today's Church

The modern church, especially in regions of affluence and comfort, faces the temptation to focus on external success while neglecting the heart of worship. The warning to Ephesus challenges us to pursue spiritual renewal through love, not merely programs or traditions. Churches are called to become communities where the love for Christ is evident in both personal devotion and collective action.

The relationship between works and love must be clear: while works are essential, they must stem from a genuine love for Christ. Faithfulness in doctrine, service, and community engagement should always flow from a place of spiritual fervor. When churches and believers return to their first love, their light will shine brightly, offering a powerful witness to a world in need of Christ.

The message to Ephesus is as relevant today as it was nearly two thousand years ago. It serves as a sobering reminder to the church to continually examine its heart. Spiritual fervor, passion for Christ, and love for others must be at the core of the Christian walk. Jesus calls each believer to return to the love that first inspired their journey of faith, and in doing so, they will find renewed purpose, power, and eternal life.

In every generation, Jesus walks among His churches, observing their deeds and searching their hearts. His words to the church at Ephesus remind us that He values both faithfulness in doctrine and fervor in love. May today's churches heed the call to remember, repent, and rekindle their first love, ensuring that their lampstands remain shining bright as witnesses to the love and truth of Jesus Christ.

Prophetic Meaning of the Church of Ephesus

The church of Ephesus represents more than just a historical congregation; it embodies a prophetic dimension that applies to various periods in church history and serves as a timeless lesson for believers today. The letter to Ephesus contains layers of prophetic meaning, from its immediate relevance to the early church to its application in future church ages, as well as a personal and spiritual message for Christians throughout the centuries.

1. The Early Apostolic Church (Prophetic Timeline)

The church of Ephesus prophetically represents the early apostolic church, which spans from the time of the apostles (around 33 AD) to the end of the first century. This was a time when the church was establishing itself amidst persecution, false teachings, and the expansion of the gospel throughout the Roman Empire. The characteristics of the Ephesian church—its hard work, patience, and ability to discern false apostles—were commendable.

During this time, the church was doctrinally sound and zealous in defending the truth of the gospel. The apostolic era is marked by evangelistic fervor, church planting, and the safeguarding of the faith against heresies, much like the Ephesians who "tested those who say they are apostles but are not" (Rev. 2:2). However, by the end of the first century, as the last apostles passed away, the early church began to lose its initial passion and love for Christ. This gradual cooling of fervor is symbolized by Ephesus losing its "first love."

2. The Loss of First Love: A Prophetic Warning

The rebuke to the Ephesian church for abandoning its first love carries a prophetic warning to all future churches and believers. As the church grew and matured, it became susceptible to the dangers of routine and institutionalization. The Ephesian church had begun to substitute religious duty and doctrinal purity for the passionate love for Christ that had characterized its earlier days.

This prophetic message is relevant to every generation: churches and believers who once burned with zeal for Christ may over time grow cold, focusing more on works and traditions than on an intimate relationship with Him. This can happen when churches become more concerned with external activities and programs rather than nurturing the heart of worship and love for Christ.

3. The Call to Repent and Return

Prophetically, Jesus' call to repent and return to the "first works" is a timeless exhortation for spiritual renewal. Throughout history, there have been periods of spiritual decline, where churches, movements, and individuals have lost the fire of their early devotion. Yet, Christ's call to Ephesus serves as a hopeful reminder that renewal and revival are always possible. Churches are given the opportunity to repent, return to their foundational love for Christ, and experience restoration.

The prophetic application of this call has been evident in various spiritual awakenings and revivals throughout history. Whether in the Reformation, the Great Awakenings, or other revival movements, the church has continually responded to the need for repentance and returning to its first love. These movements often reignite the love for Christ, restoring the fervor that had been lost through religious formalism or spiritual complacency.

4. The Removal of the Candlestick: A Prophetic Judgment

The warning that Jesus would remove the candlestick from its place if Ephesus did not repent is also prophetic of the potential consequences for any church or believer who neglects their relationship with Christ. In a broader prophetic sense, this removal can be seen as a warning to church movements or institutions that grow cold and fail to respond to Jesus' call for renewal.

Historically, many churches or denominations that were once thriving and spiritually vibrant have experienced decline or even extinction when they lost their love for Christ. Their candlestick—their influence and spiritual light—was removed, either through internal collapse or external factors. For example, many churches in regions where Christianity once flourished, such as Asia Minor (modern-day Turkey, where Ephesus was located), have since disappeared due to a combination of spiritual decline, persecution, and neglect of their first love.

This prophetic aspect of judgment reminds the church today of the urgency of maintaining a fervent relationship with Christ. Without this love, even the most active and doctrinally sound churches risk losing their effectiveness and witness.

5. The Promise to the Overcomer: Prophetic Hope

The promise to those who overcome in Ephesus—that they will eat of the tree of life in the paradise of God—

has profound prophetic significance. The tree of life symbolizes eternal life and communion with God, which was lost when humanity fell in the Garden of Eden (Genesis 3:22-24). However, Christ promises that those who overcome will regain access to this tree, indicating eternal life in the restored paradise of the new heavens and new earth (Revelation 22:2).

This promise has prophetic implications for the future state of the church and the ultimate restoration of all things. For believers, the promise of the tree of life points to the eternal inheritance awaiting the faithful. It also suggests that overcoming the challenges of spiritual coldness and returning to Christ's love are key to remaining in communion with God both now and in the life to come.

6. The Ephesus Era: A Prophetic Cycle

In a broader sense, the church of Ephesus represents a prophetic cycle that can be seen in various periods of church history. The early apostolic zeal, followed by gradual spiritual decline and the call for renewal, has repeated itself throughout the centuries. Each time the church has responded to Christ's call to return to its first love, periods of revival and renewal have followed, but each time the warning to Ephesus goes unheeded, the church risks losing its effectiveness and light.

This prophetic cycle serves as a warning to the modern church. In today's world, where there is often a focus on outward success, doctrinal correctness, and programs, the church must be careful not to lose the foundational love for Christ that fuels true worship, service, and mission. The Ephesus church era reminds us that the heart of the Christian faith is not merely in works or knowledge but in a deep, abiding love for Jesus.

The Prophetic Message of Ephesus for Today

The church of Ephesus, in its prophetic dimension, serves as a mirror for today's church. It challenges modern believers to examine whether their passion for Christ has cooled amidst the busyness of religious activity. The prophetic warning and call to repentance are as relevant now as ever, urging the church to rekindle its first love and return to the simplicity of devotion to Christ.

The prophetic promise to the overcomer offers hope: those who remain steadfast in their love for Christ, despite the temptations of apathy and spiritual decline, will partake in eternal life and fellowship with God. The tree of life in the paradise of God awaits those who overcome, promising that a vibrant, love-filled relationship with Christ will ultimately lead to eternal rewards.

The message to Ephesus calls the church, both corporately and individually, to live in a continual state of spiritual renewal, ensuring that their light remains bright and that their witness continues to glorify Christ until His return.

The prophetic significance of Ephesus is clear: love for Christ is not optional—it is the foundation of all true Christian life and ministry. Without it, even the most vibrant church will fade, but with it, the church will shine as a light in the world, drawing others to the eternal love of God.

CHAPTER 02

SMYRNA – THE PERSECUTED CHURCH

Scripture Reference: Revelation 2:8-11

Introduction to Smyrna

The church of Smyrna is unique among the seven churches of Asia, as it is one of only two that received no rebuke from Jesus. Known for its faithful endurance under persecution and poverty, Smyrna stands as a powerful example of resilience, steadfastness, and spiritual riches amid physical hardship. Jesus' message to this church highlights themes of suffering, perseverance, and divine reward.

Background on Smyrna

Smyrna, located in Asia Minor (modern-day Turkey), was a prosperous and strategically significant city in the Roman Empire. It was known for its loyalty to Rome and its involvement in emperor worship, which made it a challenging place for Christians who refused to declare allegiance to Caesar as "lord." This resistance often led to severe persecution for Smyrna's Christian community, including poverty, imprisonment, and martyrdom.

The name "Smyrna" is derived from "myrrh," a resin used for embalming, symbolizing suffering, sacrifice, and even death. This etymology is prophetically fitting, as the Christians of Smyrna would become a church associated with suffering, yet one that emitted the fragrance of faithfulness and steadfastness.

Jesus' Introduction to Smyrna

Verse 8: "And to the angel of the church in Smyrna write: 'These things says the First and the Last, who was dead, and came to life.'"

The introduction of Jesus to the Smyrna church is filled with reassurance and hope. By identifying Himself as "the First and the Last," Jesus reminds the believers that He is sovereign over time and eternity. His eternal nature assures them that He is the beginning and end of all things, including their struggles.

The phrase "who was dead, and came to life" emphasizes Jesus' power over death, a crucial message for those facing the threat of martyrdom. Jesus has conquered death, and therefore, He can offer eternal life to those who persevere. This assurance would have brought comfort to the believers in Smyrna, reminding them that even if they faced physical death, their souls were secure in Christ.

Exegetical Insights

- First and Last (G4413 – πρῶτος / prōtos; G2078 – ἔσχατος / eschatos): By using these Greek terms, Jesus identifies as eternal and sovereign, emphasizing that He is in control from the beginning to the end, providing both protection and ultimate vindication.

- Who was dead and came to life (G3498 – νεκρός / nekros; G2198 – ζάω / zaō): This phrase is not only a reminder of the resurrection but also of Jesus' triumph over death, pointing to the hope of resurrection for all believers.

The Condition of the Church at Smyrna

Verse 9: "I know your works, tribulation, and poverty (but you are rich); and I know the blasphemy of those who say they are Jews and are not, but are a synagogue of Satan."

Jesus' words, "I know your works, tribulation, and poverty," demonstrate His intimate awareness of the trials the believers in Smyrna are enduring. The church faces intense persecution, which has led to extreme poverty. Despite these physical hardships, Jesus declares that they are "rich"—rich in faith, hope, and spiritual wealth, qualities that endure beyond material possessions.

- Tribulation (G2347 – θλίψις / thlipsis): This word conveys a sense of pressure, distress, or crushing. The Christians in Smyrna are undergoing intense external pressure due to persecution, but they are enduring it faithfully.

- Poverty (G4432 – πτωχεία / ptōcheia): The believers in Smyrna suffer financial deprivation due to their faith, likely because of social and economic exclusion. Their poverty contrasts with the city's material wealth, highlighting the depth of their sacrifice.

Despite these trials, Jesus affirms their spiritual riches. This phrase aligns with passages like James 2:5, which speaks of God choosing the poor of the world to be "rich in faith." In their suffering, the Smyrnan believers are storing up treasures in heaven (Matthew 6:20), embodying the Beatitudes (Matthew 5:10-12).

The "Synagogue of Satan"

The "synagogue of Satan" refers to a group of people who claimed to be Jews but were not truly followers of God's ways. These individuals likely slandered and accused the Christians, attempting to discredit their faith and stir up persecution against them.

- Blasphemy (G988 – βλασφημία / blasphēmia): Here, it signifies slanderous or defamatory statements made against the believers. This blasphemy reflects hostility, likely rooted in religious, social, or political motivations.

- Synagogue of Satan (G4864 – συναγωγή / synagōgē): The use of "synagogue" here may indicate that some of the persecution was coming from certain Jewish groups hostile to Christians. By calling it the "synagogue of Satan," Jesus emphasizes that their actions align more with Satan's purposes than with God's.

The Call to Faithfulness Amid Suffering

Verse 10: "Do not fear any of those things which you are about to suffer. Indeed, the devil is about to throw some of you into prison, that you may be tested, and you will have tribulation ten days. Be faithful until death, and I will give you the crown of life."

Jesus tells the believers not to fear the impending trials. He warns them that some of them will face imprisonment and intense persecution as a test of their faith.

- Do not fear (G5399 – φοβέομαι / phobeomai): This phrase is a command not to be afraid, reminding the believers of the strength they have in Christ to withstand suffering.

- Tested (G3985 – πειράζω / peirazō): The trials that await them are a form of testing, a purification process intended to refine their faith.

- Tribulation for ten days: The reference to "ten days" is symbolic, possibly indicating a limited period of intense suffering. While some scholars believe it refers to literal days, others see it as a prophetic number, representing a complete but brief time of persecution.

Be Faithful Until Death

The call to be "faithful until death" is a profound invitation to perseverance. Jesus does not promise to prevent suffering, but He does assure them of a reward: the crown of life. This crown symbolizes eternal life and victory over death, echoing James 1:12, where the "crown of life" is promised to those who endure trials.

- Crown of Life (G4735 – στέφανος / stephanos): This term refers to a victor's crown, often awarded in athletic games. For the believers in Smyrna, it signifies victory over sin, death, and persecution. It is not earned by human merit but is given as a gift to those who remain faithful.

The Promise to the Overcomer

Verse 11: "He who has an ear, let him hear what the Spirit says to the churches. He who overcomes shall not be hurt by the second death."

Jesus concludes His message to Smyrna with a promise to the overcomer. The second death, as defined in Revelation 20:14, is eternal separation from God. However, those who overcome will be spared from this fate, having been faithful unto death and rewarded with eternal life.

- Second Death (G1208 – δεύτερος / deuteros; G2288 – θάνατος / thanatos): While the first death refers to physical death, the second death refers to eternal punishment. The promise of immunity from the second death underscores the eternal security of those who remain faithful in Christ.

Application for Today

The church of Smyrna teaches a timeless lesson for believers who face persecution, hardship, and opposition for their faith. Smyrna's example of steadfastness under pressure challenges Christians to remain faithful even when confronted with trials, trusting that Jesus is present and sovereign over every circumstance.

Key Takeaways

1. Faithfulness in Suffering: Believers are called to endure suffering, trusting that God uses trials to strengthen faith and produce spiritual wealth.

2. Spiritual Riches Over Material Wealth: True riches are found in a life devoted to Christ, regardless of earthly poverty.

3. Promise of Eternal Life: Jesus promises the crown of life to those who remain faithful unto death, assuring them that they will not face the second death.

The message to Smyrna reminds today's church of the cost of discipleship and the incomparable reward of eternal life with Christ. In a world where many believers face persecution, the church of Smyrna stands as a beacon of hope and a powerful call to unwavering faith.

The Church at Smyrna, one of the Seven Churches addressed in Revelation, stands out as a beacon of perseverance and faithfulness amidst persecution.

Along with Philadelphia, Smyrna is unique in that Jesus offers no rebuke to this congregation, only commendation and encouragement. This is a church that knew the cost of discipleship, having endured social, economic, and physical suffering for the sake of Christ. Jesus' message to Smyrna underscores the importance of unwavering faith in the face of tribulation and serves as an encouragement to persecuted believers throughout history.

Background on Smyrna

Smyrna, located in present-day Izmir, Turkey, was a prosperous seaport and a key center of commerce and trade in the Roman Empire. Known for its loyalty to Rome, Smyrna had a strong culture of emperor worship, which was legally enforced and created significant conflict for Christians who refused to worship Caesar. As a result, Christians in Smyrna faced exclusion, poverty, and persecution for their commitment to Christ.

The Greek word for Smyrna, Σμύρνα (G4667 – Smyrna), is derived from "myrrh," a fragrant resin used in burial rites. This etymology symbolically aligns with the church's experience, as myrrh is a symbol of suffering and death. Smyrna's persecution, however, was seasoned with the fragrance of faith, bearing witness to the church's steadfast love for Christ.

Jesus' Introduction to Smyrna

Verse 8: "And to the angel of the church in Smyrna write: 'These things says the First and the Last, who was dead, and came to life.'"

Jesus introduces Himself to the church at Smyrna with titles that emphasize His sovereignty and victory over death. By identifying as "the First and the Last" (G4413 – πρῶτος/prōtos, G2078 – ἔσχατος/eschatos), Jesus declares His eternal existence and unchanging authority over all things. This title is an affirmation of His divine identity, connecting Him with Old Testament language in Isaiah 44:6, where God Himself is called the First and the Last.

- "Who was dead, and came to life" (G3498 – νεκρός/nekros, G2198 – ζάω/zaō): This phrase serves as a profound reminder of Jesus' victory over death, a reassurance to the Smyrna believers who face the threat of martyrdom. Jesus' resurrection serves as both an assurance of eternal life for the faithful and as a reminder that suffering and death do not have the final word.

The Condition of the Church at Smyrna

Verse 9: "I know your works, tribulation, and poverty (but you are rich); and I know the blasphemy of those who say they are Jews and are not, but are a synagogue of Satan."

Jesus begins His address with the comforting words "I know," a phrase that conveys His intimate understanding of the church's struggles.

- "Works" (G2041 – ἔργον/ergon): Here, works refer to the deeds and actions of the Smyrna believers, who have demonstrated their faith through perseverance and loyalty to Christ despite persecution.

- "Tribulation" (G2347 – θλίψις/thlipsis): This Greek word denotes intense pressure or crushing, indicating the severe hardship and trials that the Smyrna church endured. Jesus acknowledges the crushing nature of their tribulations, which likely included economic deprivation, imprisonment, and even death.

- "Poverty" (G4432 – πτωχεία/ptōcheia): The church's poverty was likely due to social exclusion and economic marginalization imposed by the Roman and local authorities. While the city of Smyrna was affluent, the Christians within it were materially impoverished. Despite this, Jesus declares them to be spiritually rich, emphasizing that wealth in His kingdom is not measured by material possessions but by faithfulness and spiritual depth.

Jesus also refers to "the blasphemy of those who say they are Jews and are not, but are a synagogue of Satan." This phrase points to hostile Jewish individuals who opposed the Christians in Smyrna, accusing them and collaborating with authorities to persecute them. Jesus clarifies that, although these individuals claimed to be part of God's people, their actions aligned more closely with Satan's agenda of opposition to Christ.

The Call to Faithfulness Amid Suffering

Verse 10: "Do not fear any of those things which you are about to suffer. Indeed, the devil is about to throw some of you into prison, that you may be tested, and you will have tribulation ten days. Be faithful until death, and I will give you the crown of life."

Jesus reassures the Smyrna believers by telling them not to fear the impending trials. He explains that the devil will incite further persecution, leading to imprisonment and testing. These challenges are part of a divine testing process, purifying their faith like gold refined in fire (1 Peter 1:6-7).

- "Do not fear" (G5399 – φοβέομαι/phobeomai): This imperative commands believers to remain courageous, grounding their confidence in Christ's victory and presence.

- "Tested" (G3985 – πειράζω/peirazō): The trials they will face serve as a means of testing their faith, revealing its authenticity and strengthening their reliance on God.

- Tribulation for "ten days": The reference to ten days is often seen as a symbolic period, indicating a limited but intense time of suffering. Some scholars suggest it refers to a brief, defined period of trial, while others see it as a prophetic term symbolizing completeness in testing.

"Be faithful until death, and I will give you the crown of life."

Jesus' call for faithfulness "until death" is both a command and a promise. The crown of life (G4735 – στέφανος/stephanos) is a reward for those who endure persecution and remain loyal to Christ. Unlike a royal crown, the stephanos was a wreath awarded to victors in athletic competitions. Here, it symbolizes eternal life and victory over death, given to those who persevere. The crown of life is echoed in James 1:12, affirming God's reward for those who remain steadfast under trial.

The Promise to the Overcomer

Verse 11: "He who has an ear, let him hear what the Spirit says to the churches. He who overcomes shall not be hurt by the second death."

This promise reiterates the importance of spiritual awareness and receptivity to the Spirit's message.

- "Overcomes" (G3528 – νικάω/nikaō): To overcome here means to conquer the trials of persecution, maintaining faith in Christ despite the pressures to recant or compromise.

The Second Death

The second death (G1208 – δεύτερος/deuteros, G2288 – θάνατος/thanatos) refers to eternal separation from God, described in Revelation 20:14 as the final judgment in the lake of fire. Jesus' assurance that overcomers will not be harmed by the second death is a profound promise of eternal security for the faithful.

Application for Today

The message to Smyrna is relevant for believers today, especially for those who experience persecution and opposition. In many parts of the world, Christians face social exclusion, economic hardship, imprisonment, and even martyrdom for their faith. The call to remain faithful unto death is as applicable now as it was in the first century, reminding us of the eternal reward that awaits those who persevere.

For the persecuted church, Jesus' words to Smyrna offer encouragement and hope. The crown of life promised to those who endure is a testament to the eternal value of their sacrifices. By staying true to their faith, believers today can be assured that their suffering is not in vain and that they are storing up treasures in heaven (Matthew 6:20).

The Smyrna church's example challenges believers to evaluate their own commitment. Are we prepared to remain faithful in the face of hardship? Are we building spiritual riches, even if it means forgoing material comforts? The commendation of Smyrna emphasizes that true wealth is measured by our devotion to Christ and our willingness to endure for His sake.

The church at Smyrna stands as an enduring symbol of the power of faith in the face of suffering. Jesus' message to this church invites us to see persecution and trials not as obstacles, but as opportunities for spiritual refinement. The Smyrna believers' faithfulness, tested by fire, produced a legacy of spiritual richness and eternal reward, and the same promise holds for those who remain faithful today.

Introduction to the Prophetic Meaning of Smyrna

The prophetic significance of the church at Smyrna is a powerful testimony of faith under persecution. Historically, Smyrna represents the persecuted church era spanning from roughly A.D. 100 to 313, a time marked by severe suffering and martyrdom under Roman emperors who demanded loyalty to the imperial cult. This was a time of testing for Christians, who had to choose between faithfulness to Christ or allegiance to Caesar. Prophetically, the Smyrna church stands as a symbol of all believers who endure persecution across the ages and challenges modern Christians to stay true to their faith regardless of the cost.

Jesus' Introduction to Smyrna—A Prophetic Insight

Verse 8: "And to the angel of the church in Smyrna write: 'These things says the First and the Last, who was dead, and came to life.'"

Jesus introduces Himself to Smyrna with titles that emphasize His eternality and triumph over death. His designation as "the First and the Last" (G4413 – πρῶτος/prōtos, G2078 – ἔσχατος/eschatos) connects Jesus to the eternal, unchanging God described in Isaiah 44:6. For a persecuted church facing death, the assurance of Jesus' power over life and death provides ultimate comfort.

- "Who was dead, and came to life" (G3498 – νεκρός/nekros, G2198 – ζάω/zaō): This phrase not only affirms Jesus' victory over death but serves as a prophetic message to believers who face martyrdom. Jesus' resurrection assures them that death is not the end, and they will share in His resurrection (Romans 6:5, 2 Timothy 2:11).

Prophetic Condition of Smyrna—The Persecuted Church Era

Verse 9: "I know your works, tribulation, and poverty (but you are rich); and I know the blasphemy of those who say they are Jews and are not, but are a synagogue of Satan."

The prophetic interpretation of Smyrna reflects the intense persecution faced by early Christians, particularly in the second and third centuries. Believers in this era were systematically oppressed, yet they remained spiritually rich—a characteristic Jesus recognizes.

- "Works" (G2041 – ἔργον/ergon): The works of Smyrna's believers represent the faithfulness and spiritual endurance demonstrated under severe trials. This prophetic era is marked by the works of the early martyrs who endured suffering to uphold their faith.

- "Tribulation" (G2347 – θλίψις/thlipsis): This word describes the pressure and crushing weight of persecution, representing the broader historical suffering of Christians under Roman rule. The prophetic relevance here includes not only physical persecution but societal exclusion, as early

Christians were marginalized for rejecting the state-sanctioned religion.

- "Poverty" (G4432 – πτωχεία/ptōcheia): This likely reflects the economic hardship endured by Christians who refused to participate in idolatrous practices, resulting in their social and economic exclusion. Despite their material poverty, they were spiritually "rich," demonstrating that their value lay in eternal treasures rather than worldly wealth.

- "Synagogue of Satan": The phrase refers to those who claimed to be God's people but opposed Christ's followers, persecuting them instead of honoring God's kingdom. Prophetically, this reflects the challenges that true believers face from both external enemies and those who appear religious but work against the purposes of God.

The Call to Prophetic Faithfulness and Perseverance

Verse 10: "Do not fear any of those things which you are about to suffer. Indeed, the devil is about to throw some of you into prison, that you may be tested, and you will have tribulation ten days. Be faithful until death, and I will give you the crown of life."

The prophetic meaning of Smyrna's call to faithfulness reveals an important message for all ages, but particularly for Christians under duress. Jesus encourages Smyrna to fear not, highlighting the need for courage amidst trials that believers may encounter throughout history.

- "Fear not" (G5399 – φοβέομαι/phobeomai): Jesus' command not to fear is a prophetic call to boldness for all believers who face the threat of persecution. Fearlessness is an essential component of faithful endurance.

- "Tribulation ten days": The ten days are often seen prophetically as a defined period of trial. Some theologians interpret these ten days as symbolic of a specific period of testing for the persecuted church in history, possibly pointing to the ten major waves of Roman persecution from Emperor Nero to Diocletian. Others interpret it as a complete but limited season, reminding believers that God sovereignly limits the duration of their suffering.

"Be faithful until death, and I will give you the crown of life."

The prophetic message for Smyrna includes the promise of the crown of life (G4735 – στέφανος/stephanos), which symbolizes victory and eternal life. For believers in the persecuted church era—and for all who face trials for their faith—this crown represents God's promise of eternal reward for those who remain steadfast. This prophetic promise encourages believers to view earthly suffering through the lens of eternity, with the crown of life as their ultimate reward.

The Promise to the Overcomer—Prophetic Assurance

Verse 11: "He who has an ear, let him hear what the Spirit says to the churches. He who overcomes shall not be hurt by the second death."

The prophetic significance of Jesus' words to Smyrna carries eternal weight. Overcomers are promised immunity from the second death (G1208 – δεύτερος/deuteros, G2288 – θάνατος/thanatos), a term that refers to the final judgment and eternal separation from God, described in Revelation 20:14. For those who endure suffering and persecution for Christ, this is a profound assurance that they will be spared from spiritual death.

- "He who overcomes" (G3528 – νικάω/nikaō): Overcoming in this context means remaining faithful to Christ, no matter the opposition or persecution faced. The prophetic message here offers hope, signifying the eternal victory reserved for those who hold fast to their faith despite trials.

Prophetic Application for Today

The church at Smyrna represents believers throughout history who endure persecution for their faith, but its prophetic application remains vital for today's global church. In many parts of the world, Christians face imprisonment, social marginalization, and even martyrdom for their loyalty to Christ. The message to Smyrna underscores that while persecution is inevitable, it serves as a refining fire that strengthens faith and purifies devotion.

For modern believers in contexts where persecution is subtle but present, Smyrna's example reminds us to examine the depth of our faith and our readiness to endure hardship for the gospel. Even in a world that may not demand allegiance to an emperor, believers face societal pressures to conform. The prophetic message of Smyrna challenges us to hold our allegiance to Christ above all else, finding courage in His promise of resurrection and eternal life.

Concluding Reflections on Smyrna's Prophetic Message

The prophetic message to Smyrna is both timeless and profoundly relevant. Jesus' words are a call to steadfastness for all believers who face trials for their faith, reminding them of the eternal reward that awaits those who persevere. Smyrna's prophetic significance extends to every Christian who is tested by persecution, whether severe or subtle, offering the assurance that Christ, who was dead and came to life, stands with us in every trial.

In a world where allegiance to Christ often leads to opposition, the church at Smyrna prophetically points us toward the eternal perspective: the promise of the crown of life and the certainty of God's presence with us through every test. As we heed this prophetic message, we are reminded that suffering for Christ is not in vain, for He will bring us through to eternal life.

CHAPTER 03

PERGAMUN – THE COMPROMISING CHURCH

Scripture Reference: Revelation 2:12-17

Introduction to Pergamum

Pergamum was one of the most prominent cities of ancient Asia Minor, known for its wealth, intellectual culture, and religious diversity. As the center of multiple pagan temples, including those dedicated to Zeus, Athena, and the emperor cult, Pergamum earned the reputation of being "Satan's throne," as noted in the Book of Revelation. The church in Pergamum faced the constant pressure of being surrounded by idolatrous practices, and while they remained steadfast in some areas, they compromised in others.

Jesus' Introduction to Pergamum—The Sword of Judgment

Verse 12: "And to the angel of the church in Pergamum write: 'These are the words of him who has the sharp, double-edged sword.'"

Jesus introduces Himself to Pergamum with a powerful image: the sharp, double-edged sword (G4501 – ῥομφαία/rhompheia), signifying His authority to judge and divide truth from falsehood. In Hebrews 4:12, the Word of God is described as sharper than any two-edged sword, capable of discerning the thoughts and intents of the heart. Here, the double-edged sword represents Jesus' discernment and judgment, particularly pertinent to a church struggling with compromise.

This imagery is a reminder to Pergamum that Jesus sees beyond outward loyalty and can discern the internal compromises of the heart. The sword is both a warning and a reminder that the truth cannot coexist with error in His kingdom.

The Condition of Pergamum—Commendation Amidst Opposition

Verse 13: "I know where you live—where Satan has his throne. Yet you remain true to my name. You did not renounce your faith in me, not even in the days of Antipas, my faithful witness, who was put to death in your city—where Satan lives."

Jesus begins His message with a commendation, acknowledging the challenging spiritual climate in which the believers in Pergamum exist.

- "Satan's throne": This phrase could refer to Pergamum's pagan altars and the intense emperor worship demanded in the city. The phrase underscores the demonic influence and opposition that Christians faced in a culture so entrenched in idolatry and false worship.

- "You remain true to my name" (G3686 – ὄνομα/onoma): Despite their circumstances, the believers held fast to their faith and did not deny the name of Christ. The church was willing to stand for Christ, even at great personal risk, showing their commitment to the truth of the gospel.

- Antipas, my faithful witness: Antipas is identified as a martyr for his faith in Christ, known for his unwavering loyalty even to the point of death. He exemplifies what it means to be a "faithful witness" (G3144 – μάρτυς/martys), which is derived from the same Greek root as "martyr." Jesus commends Antipas, and by extension, the entire church, for their courage in the face of persecution.

The Compromise of Pergamum—Tolerance of False Teachings

Verse 14: "Nevertheless, I have a few things against you: You have people there who hold to the teaching of Balaam, who taught Balak to entice the Israelites to sin so that they ate food sacrificed to idols and committed sexual immorality."

In contrast to their faithfulness in persecution, Pergamum is rebuked for compromising with false teachings, which allowed sin to creep into the church.

- Teaching of Balaam (G903 – Βαλαάμ/Balaam): Balaam was an Old Testament prophet who led the Israelites into idolatry and immorality (Numbers 31:16). Here, the "doctrine of Balaam" refers to teaching that encourages compromise with sin, particularly idolatry and immorality. The prophetic implication is that certain believers in Pergamum were adopting pagan practices, weakening their devotion to Christ.

- Eating food sacrificed to idols (G1494 – εἰδωλόθυτος/eidolothytos) and sexual immorality (G4202 – πορνεία/porneia): These practices were common in pagan rituals, and the acceptance of such actions within the church indicated a serious moral and spiritual compromise. By tolerating these practices, the church risked diluting its commitment to holiness and purity.

Verse 15: "Likewise, you also have those who hold to the teaching of the Nicolaitans."

The Nicolaitans (G3531 – Νικολαΐτης/Nikolaitēs) represented another group within the church teaching practices that encouraged compromise with pagan culture. Although the exact nature of their doctrine is debated, it likely involved a similar blend of idolatry and immorality. The prophetic message here warns against any teachings that justify sin under the guise of tolerance or cultural conformity.

Call to Repentance—The Sword of Judgment as a Warning

Verse 16: "Repent therefore! Otherwise, I will soon come to you and will fight against them with the sword of my mouth."

Jesus' call to repent (G3340 – μετανοέω/metanoeō) is urgent and necessary for a church that is veering toward spiritual complacency. The call to repentance signifies a complete turning away from compromise and a renewed commitment to holiness and obedience.

- "Sword of my mouth": The prophetic warning underscores the reality of Christ's judgment on those who choose compromise over faithfulness. Just as the Word of God is able to discern the truth and pierce through deception, Jesus warns that He will confront the false teachings and moral laxity within the church.

The judgment here is not just about external correction but also involves Christ's discernment in addressing the heart and intent behind these actions.

The Promise to the Overcomer—Hidden Manna and a White Stone

Verse 17: "He who has an ear, let him hear what the Spirit says to the churches. To the one who overcomes, I will give some of the hidden manna. I will also give that person a white stone with a new name written on it, known only to the one who receives it."

For those who resist compromise, Jesus offers a promise filled with profound symbolic meaning.

- Hidden manna (G3131 – μάννα/manna): Manna represents God's supernatural provision, recalling how He provided for Israel in the wilderness. For believers, hidden manna symbolizes the spiritual nourishment and strength that come from a relationship with Christ. In contrast to the food offered in pagan sacrifices, Jesus promises true, sustaining spiritual sustenance.

- White stone (G5586 – ψῆφος/psēphos): In ancient courts, white stones were often used as tokens of acquittal, while black stones indicated condemnation. A white stone represents purity, acceptance, and an assured place in God's presence. This prophetic promise reflects the purity and victory that await those who maintain their loyalty to Christ.

- New name (G3686 – ὄνομα/onoma): Receiving a new name signifies a new identity and intimate relationship with Christ, marking the believer as belonging to God. This new name, known only to the recipient, represents the unique and personal relationship each believer has with Jesus.

Prophetic Application for Today's Church

The church of Pergamum is a reminder for today's church to avoid compromise with the surrounding culture. In a world where tolerance is often valued over truth, the call to Pergamum speaks directly to the modern believer: hold fast to the truth, even if it means standing against popular opinion.

In practical terms, this means that believers are called to discern the influences within their church and personal life, ensuring that they align with God's Word rather than societal norms. Compromise may offer temporary relief, but it leads to spiritual weakness. Pergamum's message encourages Christians to remain steadfast, maintaining both truth and love in a world where they are often pitted against each other.

Concluding Reflections on Pergamum

Pergamum's prophetic message is both a warning and a promise. It serves as a powerful reminder that faithfulness to Christ requires vigilance and discernment, especially in matters of doctrine and morality. Jesus' promise of hidden manna and a white stone assures believers that He will provide for those who overcome, granting them eternal sustenance, purity, and a place in His kingdom.

For every believer today, Pergamum's message calls us to examine our hearts, identify areas of compromise, and renew our commitment to live out our faith with conviction and purity.

Pergamum, an influential City in Ancient Asia Minor, was a Center of Cultural, Political, and Religious Power.

It housed famous pagan temples to gods such as Zeus and Asclepius, and the city was a hub for emperor worship, which often pressured residents to declare allegiance to Rome's deified leaders. This culturally rich but spiritually dark environment posed significant challenges for the believers in Pergamum, who were commended for their loyalty but also rebuked for their compromises with the prevailing idolatry.

Jesus' Introduction to Pergamum—The Sword of Judgment

Verse 12: "And to the angel of the church in Pergamum write: 'These are the words of him who has the sharp, double-edged sword.'"

Jesus introduces Himself to the church at Pergamum with a powerful symbol—the "sharp, double-edged sword"

(Greek: ῥομφαία, rhomphaia, Strong's G4501). This sword is representative of divine authority, judgment, and discernment. As described in Hebrews 4:12, God's word is living, powerful, and sharper than any two-edged sword, capable of discerning thoughts and intentions. By using this image, Jesus emphasizes His power to expose and judge both faithfulness and sin within the church.

This sword image serves as both a warning and a reminder. While the church was commended for its faithfulness in holding to Jesus' name, the sword of judgment is a sobering reminder that true faith must remain uncompromised.

The Condition of Pergamum—Commendation Amidst Opposition

Verse 13: "I know where you live—where Satan has his throne. Yet you remain true to my name. You did not renounce your faith in me, not even in the days of Antipas, my faithful witness, who was put to death in your city—where Satan lives."

Jesus acknowledges that the believers in Pergamum reside in a particularly dark environment, "where Satan's throne" exists. This phrase likely refers to the high level of pagan worship, including the emperor cult, which dominated Pergamum.

- "Where Satan has his throne": This phrase underscores the intense spiritual opposition that surrounded the believers in Pergamum. The phrase suggests that the influence of pagan worship and emperor reverence created an environment hostile to Christian faith and morality.

- Holding fast to His name: Despite these pressures, the church is commended for its loyalty to Christ's name. The term for "name" (Greek: ὄνομα, onoma, Strong's G3686) reflects identity and allegiance. To hold to Jesus' name means the church did not renounce Him or His teachings, even when doing so put their lives at risk.

- Antipas, my faithful witness: Jesus singles out Antipas, who was martyred for his unwavering commitment to the faith. The Greek term for "witness" (μάρτυς, martys, Strong's G3144) is the root of the English word "martyr." Antipas' steadfastness in the face of death serves as a model for all believers facing persecution.

The Compromise of Pergamum—Tolerance of False Teachings

Verse 14: "Nevertheless, I have a few things against you: You have people there who hold to the teaching of Balaam, who taught Balak to entice the Israelites to sin so that they ate food sacrificed to idols and committed sexual immorality."

While the church maintained some elements of faithfulness, Jesus rebukes them for tolerating teachings that compromised their purity.

- Teaching of Balaam: Balaam, an Old Testament figure, is known for leading Israel into idolatry and immorality through compromise with pagan practices (Numbers 31:16). The term used for "teaching" (διδαχή, didachē, Strong's G1322) refers to the act of promoting doctrine. This compromise allowed cultural and moral practices contrary to God's commands to influence the church.

- Eating food sacrificed to idols and sexual immorality (εἰδωλόθυτος, eidōlothytos, Strong's G1494; πορνεία, porneia, Strong's G4202): These practices were common in pagan worship rituals. Allowing these practices blurred the church's distinctiveness and holiness, diluting their witness and fellowship with God. The mention of idolatry and immorality also suggests a broader moral drift that prioritized acceptance over adherence to biblical standards.

Verse 15: "Likewise, you also have those who hold to the teaching of the Nicolaitans."

The Nicolaitans (Greek: Νικολαΐτης, Nikolaitēs, Strong's G3531) were a sect believed to advocate similar forms of compromise, including moral laxity and integration of pagan practices. Although details of their doctrine are not explicit, they represented a faction that sought to accommodate paganism within Christian practice, further weakening the church's stand for truth.

Call to Repentance—The Sword of Judgment as a Warning

Verse 16: "Repent therefore! Otherwise, I will soon come to you and will fight against them with the sword of my mouth."

Jesus calls the church to repent (μετανοέω, metanoeō, Strong's G3340), a term signifying a complete change of mind and direction. Repentance here implies turning away from compromise and realigning with God's standards.

- Sword of my mouth: The repeated reference to the "sword" (ῥομφαία, rhomphaia, Strong's G4501) is significant. In this context, the "sword of my mouth" symbolizes Jesus' power to discern and judge by His word (Hebrews 4:12). It suggests that divine truth will confront and expose error. Those who continue in compromise will be judged by the very Word they claim to uphold.

The prophetic warning is that judgment begins in the house of God (1 Peter 4:17). When believers tolerate what is contrary to God's will, they risk the sharp rebuke of the One who holds ultimate authority over the church.

The Promise to the Overcomer—Hidden Manna and a White Stone

Verse 17: "He who has an ear, let him hear what the Spirit says to the churches. To the one who overcomes, I will give some of the hidden manna. I will also give that person a white stone with a new name written on it, known only to the one who receives it."

For those who resist compromise, Jesus promises rewards with deep symbolic meaning:

- Hidden manna (μάννα, manna, Strong's G3131): Manna, God's supernatural provision for Israel in the wilderness, represents sustenance and divine fellowship. The "hidden" aspect implies that the church will receive a deeper, spiritual provision unknown to the world. This hidden manna contrasts with the food sacrificed to idols, signifying a purer, divine sustenance in fellowship with Christ.

- White stone (ψῆφος, psēphos, Strong's G5586): In ancient times, a white stone was used as a symbol of acquittal in a trial or a token of honor. The white stone here represents purity, acceptance, and approval from God. It assures the believer of Christ's approval and their place in His kingdom.

- New name (ὄνομα, onoma, Strong's G3686): The promise of a new name reflects the believer's transformed identity in Christ. Known only to the recipient, it suggests an intimate, unique relationship between Christ and the individual, marking them as His own.

Application for Today: Guarding Against Compromise

The message to the church at Pergamum holds critical lessons for believers today, particularly concerning the dangers of spiritual compromise. The prophetic word to Pergamum cautions against diluting the faith in a culture that often pressures believers to conform. Many modern-day challenges mirror those faced by Pergamum, as Christians navigate cultural acceptance without compromising core biblical values.

The prophetic application of this message for today's church is clear:

1. Stand Firm in Faithfulness: In a world that often promotes relative truth, believers are called to stand firm in their commitment to Christ's teachings, rejecting influences that contradict God's Word.

2. Reject Moral Compromise: The call to holiness requires vigilance in maintaining purity, both morally and doctrinally. Compromising in these areas leads to a diluted witness and hinders the church's effectiveness.

3. Embrace the Promise of Eternal Fellowship: Like the "hidden manna" and "white stone," the ultimate reward for faithfulness is eternal fellowship with Christ, a reward far greater than any temporal approval or acceptance.

The prophetic message to Pergamum is a call to all believers to examine their lives, purify their worship, and remain true to the gospel despite cultural pressures. In doing so, the promise of divine acceptance, spiritual sustenance, and eternal reward awaits.

The Prophetic Meaning of Pergamum in Today's Church

The message to Pergamum highlights a cautionary prophecy relevant for today: the dangers of compromise within Christianity and the critical need for remaining true to biblical teachings. Pergamum, positioned in an environment of pagan influences, is emblematic of a church that wrestles with loyalty to Christ amid cultural and spiritual pressures to conform. In a world where secular beliefs and societal trends challenge traditional biblical values, Pergamum represents the ongoing struggle between steadfast faith and accommodation to the surrounding culture.

Pergamum's Prophetic Symbolism—A Warning Against Spiritual Compromise

The church in Pergamum was commended for holding fast to the name of Jesus despite being "where Satan's throne is" (Revelation 2:13), referring to a society deeply entrenched in idolatry and false religions. However,

Pergamum tolerated the influence of corrupt doctrines, like the teachings of Balaam and the Nicolaitans, that encouraged moral laxity and idolatry. This tolerance eroded the church's witness and threatened its purity, providing a prophetic warning for Christians today to resist compromising core truths in the face of cultural or societal pressures.

1. The Doctrine of Balaam as a Symbol of Compromise: The "doctrine of Balaam" (Numbers 22–25; Revelation 2:14) symbolizes teachings that seduce believers into compromising their faith for worldly gain or acceptance. Balaam, an Old Testament prophet, led Israel to sin through alliances that introduced idolatry and immorality, weakening Israel's relationship with God. Today, this doctrine is reflected when churches or believers compromise biblical truths, accepting ideologies or practices that conflict with Scripture in order to be more culturally relevant or inclusive. This could manifest in ways such as diluting biblical doctrines on marriage, morality, or the exclusivity of salvation through Christ.

2. The Nicolaitan Doctrine and Spiritual Erosion: The Nicolaitan teaching promoted a distorted sense of grace that encouraged moral permissiveness. This doctrine warns against the gradual acceptance of behaviors or beliefs that lead Christians away from biblical standards. Modern parallels include the growing acceptance of doctrines that downplay

the significance of repentance, sanctification, and obedience in the Christian life. This erosion allows secular ethics to enter Christian spaces, creating a spiritual disconnect from God's Word.

Modern Challenges and the Urgent Call for Faithfulness

In today's world, Christians encounter philosophies and lifestyles that can subtly shift focus from a Christ-centered faith to a more secular, self-centered form of spirituality. For instance:

- Relativism: The increasing normalization of "relative truth" pressures Christians to soften the exclusivity of biblical truths, leading some to view all beliefs as equally valid, which conflicts with the gospel's call for distinct, uncompromising allegiance to Christ (John 14:6).

- Tolerance of Sinful Practices: Some churches may increasingly adopt practices or values that contradict Scripture, blurring the lines between holiness and worldliness (2 Corinthians 6:17). This tolerance can lead to a lack of accountability within the church, where sin is no longer addressed according to biblical standards.

- Pressure to Conform: As culture advances, Christians may feel pressured to conform to societal expectations that conflict with Scripture. Pergamum's struggle highlights the prophetic danger of allowing societal norms to redefine faith, which can lead to a weakened relationship with God.

The Call to Repent and Hold Fast

The prophetic call to Pergamum serves as a reminder for Christians today to return to the uncompromised truth of God's Word. Jesus' instruction to "repent" (Revelation 2:16) is not only a call to the church of Pergamum but to all believers to realign with Scripture and reject any teaching or behavior that strays from God's will. Jesus warns that failing to repent will result in the sword of His mouth bringing judgment, underscoring the urgency for Christians to examine their beliefs and practices in light of biblical truth.

- Renewed Devotion to Scripture: The solution for avoiding compromise is a steadfast commitment to Scripture. A renewed devotion to biblical study, prayer, and fellowship strengthens the church's ability to discern truth from falsehood and empowers believers to stand firm.

- Accountability within the Church: Pergamum's compromise highlights the need for accountability within Christian communities. Leaders and congregations alike must uphold biblical standards, fostering environments that resist compromise and promote spiritual growth.

- Living as "Salt and Light": Believers are called to be distinct, living as "salt and light" in the world (Matthew 5:13-

16). Pergamum's prophetic message urges Christians to maintain their unique identity, prioritizing allegiance to Christ over societal acceptance.

The Reward for Overcoming Compromise

The promise to the overcomer in Pergamum speaks to all believers facing the temptation to compromise. Jesus promises "hidden manna" and a "white stone with a new name" (Revelation 2:17), symbols of divine provision, intimacy with God, and assured identity in Christ. The hidden manna represents spiritual nourishment from God, a provision that surpasses any worldly gain derived from compromise. The white stone signifies acceptance and approval from God, affirming the believer's identity and eternal relationship with Him.

Application of Pergamum's Message for Today's Believers

The prophetic message to Pergamum is an urgent reminder to today's church:

- Vigilance Against Compromise: The church must guard against teachings or practices that dilute biblical truths, embracing discernment through consistent engagement with Scripture.

- Renewed Zeal for Holiness: Pergamum's example urges Christians to uphold purity in doctrine and life, valuing holiness and obedience to God as central to faith.

- Faithful Witness: In a culture that often challenges biblical values, Pergamum's story encourages believers to remain a faithful witness, unashamedly standing for Christ even when it goes against popular opinion.

Pergamum's prophetic message challenges believers to choose uncompromised allegiance to Christ, promising eternal rewards for those who endure. The church's call today is to resist the allure of acceptance at the expense of truth, upholding Scripture's authority as the guiding standard for faith and life. Through the lessons of Pergamum, Christians are empowered to live distinct, faithful lives, standing as a testimony to God's unchanging truth.

CHAPTER 04

THYATIRA-THE CHURCH OF FALSE PROPHETS

Scripture Reference: Revelation 2:18-29

Introduction

The church at Thyatira was unique among the seven churches of Asia Minor in its combination of strong service and growth with a significant tolerance of false prophecy. Jesus commends the church for its works, love, service, and patience, acknowledging that its deeds had even grown stronger with time. However, the church tolerated a destructive influence, symbolized by "Jezebel," a false prophetess who led members into idolatry and immorality. This duality in the church of Thyatira—exemplary service marred by permissiveness toward false teaching—offers valuable insights for Christians today. In this chapter, we'll delve deeply into the specific issues Jesus addressed with

Thyatira, their prophetic implications, and the modern-day applications of this message.

Thyatira's Commendation: A Church of Growth and Service

In Revelation 2:18, Jesus identifies Himself as "the Son of God, who has eyes like a flame of fire, and His feet like fine brass." This vivid imagery of Christ emphasizes His divine authority, penetrating vision, and unyielding judgment. Jesus first acknowledges the positive traits of the church in Thyatira, affirming its growth in faith and deeds.

- "I know thy works, and charity, and service, and faith, and thy patience, and thy works; and the last to be more than the first." (Revelation 2:19)

- Works (Greek: ergon, Strong's G2041): Denotes a broad range of actions, including good deeds and labors done in faith.

- Charity (Greek: agape, Strong's G26): Refers to love in its highest form, suggesting that Thyatira was a church motivated by love.

- Service (Greek: diakonia, Strong's G1248): Implies active ministry, reflecting the church's commitment to serving others.

- Patience (Greek: hypomone, Strong's G5281): Represents endurance under trial, showing the resilience of the church in faith and works.

Jesus commends Thyatira for these qualities, which were not only present but growing stronger. Unlike some other churches, Thyatira was not stagnant; its commitment to service and faith was increasing, representing an active and thriving Christian community.

The Reproof: Tolerating the Spirit of Jezebel

Despite its strengths, Thyatira allowed a false prophetess, symbolically referred to as "Jezebel," to promote practices that were antithetical to the gospel.

- "Notwithstanding, I have a few things against thee, because thou sufferest that woman Jezebel, which calleth herself a prophetess, to teach and to seduce my servants to commit fornication, and to eat things sacrificed unto idols." (Revelation 2:20)

- Jezebel: This is likely a symbolic reference to the infamous queen in the Old Testament who led Israel into idolatry and immorality (1 Kings 16:31). She epitomizes rebellion against God and the seduction of His people away from holiness.

- Fornication (Greek: porneia, Strong's G4202): Used here both literally and symbolically, referring to sexual immorality and spiritual unfaithfulness.

- Idolatry: Thyatira's tolerance of Jezebel's teaching suggests a blending of Christian doctrine with pagan practices, likely linked to the local trade guilds, which often included idol worship as part of their activities.

Jezebel's influence was spiritually destructive, promoting compromise and moral corruption within the church. By tolerating her teaching, the church allowed sin to gain a foothold, leading many believers astray.

The Call to Repentance and the Warning of Judgment

Jesus calls Thyatira to repentance, warning of serious consequences if they do not turn from these teachings.

- "And I gave her space to repent of her fornication; and she repented not." (Revelation 2:21)

- This verse reveals Jesus' patience, as He gave Jezebel time to repent. However, her unwillingness to turn from her sins makes the impending judgment inevitable.

- "Behold, I will cast her into a bed, and them that commit adultery with her into great tribulation, except they repent of their deeds." (Revelation 2:22)

- Cast her into a bed: This phrase, a powerful image, likely symbolizes sickness or death as a consequence of her sins.

- Great tribulation (Greek: thlipsis megale, Strong's G2347 and G3173): This signifies severe hardship and distress, often seen as divine punishment.

- Adultery (Greek: moicheia, Strong's G3430): Here, spiritual unfaithfulness is equated with adultery, depicting the betrayal of one's relationship with God.

The strong warning to Jezebel and her followers reveals the serious consequences of doctrinal and moral compromise within the church. Jesus emphasizes that He will deal with all parties involved unless they repent, signifying the need for a pure and unadulterated faith.

The Reward for Faithful Overcomers

For those in Thyatira who remain faithful, Jesus promises a reward that contrasts with the judgment reserved for those who follow Jezebel.

- "But unto you I say, and unto the rest in Thyatira, as many as have not this doctrine, and which have not known the depths of Satan, as they speak; I will put upon you none other burden." (Revelation 2:24)

- Jesus acknowledges that not everyone in Thyatira has fallen into Jezebel's teachings. He promises not to add further burdens on those who have remained true to the faith.

- "And he that overcometh, and keepeth my works unto the end, to him will I give power over the nations." (Revelation 2:26)

- Overcometh (Greek: nikao, Strong's G3528): Refers to achieving victory over sin, the world, and false teachings.

- Power over the nations: This phrase is a promise of authority, reflecting the future rule of the faithful alongside Christ in His kingdom (Psalm 2:8-9).

- "And I will give him the morning star." (Revelation 2:28)

- Morning Star: Often associated with Christ Himself (Revelation 22:16), this symbolizes guidance, hope, and the ultimate reward of fellowship with Jesus.

The Prophetic Meaning of Thyatira: A Warning to Avoid Doctrinal Compromise

Thyatira prophetically symbolizes the dangers that arise when a church allows false teaching to infiltrate its midst. Today, many churches face similar pressures to conform to secular ideologies or to tolerate practices contrary to Scripture. The message to Thyatira serves as a call for the church to maintain doctrinal purity and resist the influence of teachings that lead believers away from the truth.

1. False Prophets and Doctrines: Just as Jezebel led Thyatira astray, modern "Jezebels" represent any influences or teachings that pull believers away from biblical truth. Churches today must be vigilant against accepting doctrines that distort the gospel.

2. The Danger of Tolerance: Thyatira tolerated Jezebel, and this tolerance had damaging effects. Jesus' warning reminds us that unchecked tolerance of sin and false teaching ultimately erodes a church's spiritual foundation.

3. Faithfulness Brings Reward: To the faithful in Thyatira, Jesus promises the "morning star," symbolizing the glory of an eternal relationship with Him. This promise encourages believers today to cling to truth, assured of the reward awaiting those who endure.

Application for Today's Church

The message to Thyatira is a call for today's church to remain vigilant, recognizing the destructive potential of false teachings and moral compromise. Churches must exercise discernment, address sin, and prioritize the truth of Scripture, even when faced with societal pressures that encourage tolerance and inclusivity at the cost of spiritual integrity. Thyatira's lesson underscores the importance of unwavering allegiance to Christ and a commitment to holiness.

Key Takeaways:

- Uphold doctrinal purity and resist teachings that distort the gospel.

- Address sin and compromise directly, avoiding tolerance of influences that threaten the church's integrity.

- Embrace the promise of eternal reward and the privilege of reigning with Christ as a motivation for remaining faithful.

The church of Thyatira serves as both a warning and an encouragement, highlighting the need for resilience against compromise and the assurance of God's reward for those who are steadfast.

The Church of Thyatira, like many Churches today, struggled with the balance between commendable deeds and tolerating false teachings.

Known for its love, service, faith, and patience, Thyatira's commendation from Jesus highlights its significant growth in good works. Yet, beneath this faithfulness lay a troubling acceptance of a false prophetess, symbolically called "Jezebel." Her influence led believers into idolatry and immorality, drawing them away from God's commands and truth. In this chapter, we'll explore Thyatira's message and uncover its timeless applications, using strong concordance references for a more profound and contextual understanding.

The Commendation of Thyatira: Growing in Good Works

The letter to the church in Thyatira begins with a powerful image of Jesus Christ, emphasizing His authority and piercing judgment.

- "These things saith the Son of God, who hath His eyes like unto a flame of fire, and His feet are like fine brass." (Revelation 2:18)

- Eyes like a flame of fire: This description symbolizes Jesus' ability to see beyond appearances into the heart, discerning thoughts, intentions, and hidden deeds. The imagery conveys the purity and strength of His judgment, representing His ability to expose sin and purify the church.

- Feet like fine brass: Brass, or bronze, symbolizes strength and durability, often associated with judgment in the Bible. Here, it suggests that Christ's judgments are both pure and unwavering, ready to withstand and correct any form of corruption.

Qualities of Thyatira

- "I know thy works, and charity, and service, and faith, and thy patience, and thy works; and the last to be more than the first." (Revelation 2:19)

- Works (Greek: ergon, Strong's G2041): Refers to acts of service and righteousness, highlighting the church's active involvement in doing good.

- Charity (Greek: agape, Strong's G26): The highest form of love, reflecting Thyatira's loving character toward others and God.

- Service (Greek: diakonia, Strong's G1248): Indicates ministry or acts of help, showing the church's commitment to aiding others and meeting their needs.

- Faith (Greek: pistis, Strong's G4102): Their deep trust in Christ led them to sustain good works and withstand challenges.

- Patience (Greek: hypomone, Strong's G5281): Endurance under trials, suggesting that Thyatira was resilient and persistent, growing stronger in their faith and actions over time.

The Reproof: Tolerating False Teaching and Idolatry

Despite these virtues, Thyatira allowed a destructive influence, referred to symbolically as "Jezebel," a figure associated with idolatry and immorality.

- "Notwithstanding, I have a few things against thee, because thou sufferest that woman Jezebel, which calleth herself a prophetess, to teach and to seduce my servants to commit fornication, and to eat things sacrificed unto idols." (Revelation 2:20)

- Sufferest (Greek: eao, Strong's G1439): Means to tolerate or allow; here, it implies that the church permitted Jezebel's influence without challenging it.

- Jezebel: This reference likely evokes the Old Testament queen who led Israel into idolatry (1 Kings 16:31-33). Jezebel symbolizes a corrupting force within the church, encouraging behavior contrary to God's standards.

- Fornication (Greek: porneia, Strong's G4202): Symbolizes both physical immorality and spiritual unfaithfulness, as Thyatira's members were led into practices incompatible with Christian teaching.

- Eating things sacrificed to idols: Reflects a common pagan practice, involving participation in feasts honoring other gods. This was considered a form of idolatry and spiritual compromise.

Jezebel's influence was insidious, leading believers away from God. By tolerating her presence, the church of Thyatira allowed sin to enter and fester, weakening its spiritual foundation and causing believers to stumble in their faith.

The Call to Repentance and the Consequences of Rejection

Jesus, with eyes like a flame of fire, sees not only the good but also the sin in Thyatira. He provides an opportunity for repentance but warns of severe consequences if they continue down this path.

- "And I gave her space to repent of her fornication; and she repented not." (Revelation 2:21)

- Space to repent: This phrase indicates that Jesus, in His patience, offered Jezebel a chance to turn from her ways. His long-suffering demonstrates His desire for repentance and restoration rather than immediate judgment.

- "Behold, I will cast her into a bed, and them that commit adultery with her into great tribulation, except they repent of their deeds." (Revelation 2:22)

- Cast her into a bed: Symbolic of punishment or suffering, implying that her actions would bring her and her followers severe consequences.

- Great tribulation (Greek: thlipsis megale, Strong's G2347 and G3173): Suggests significant hardship and distress, often interpreted as divine judgment on those who continue in sin without repentance.

- Adultery (Greek: moicheia, Strong's G3430): Represents betrayal, particularly of a spiritual nature, as those who followed Jezebel compromised their covenant with God.

Jesus warns that judgment will befall all who participate in Jezebel's sins, underscoring the seriousness of false teaching and the spiritual unfaithfulness it causes.

The Reward for the Faithful Remnant

For those in Thyatira who remain faithful and refuse Jezebel's teachings, Jesus promises rewards of authority and fellowship.

- "But unto you I say, and unto the rest in Thyatira, as many as have not this doctrine, and which have not known the depths of Satan, as they speak; I will put upon you none other burden." (Revelation 2:24)

- Depths of Satan: A reference to the hidden, corrupt knowledge promoted by Jezebel, which was believed to reveal deeper spiritual truths but instead led believers into deception.

- No other burden: This indicates Jesus' compassion for the faithful. He recognizes the challenges they face and assures them that His expectations are reasonable and achievable.

- "And he that overcometh, and keepeth my works unto the end, to him will I give power over the nations." (Revelation 2:26)

- Overcometh (Greek: nikao, Strong's G3528): Victory over sin, the world, and false teachings, achieved by faithfulness to Christ.

- Power over the nations: A prophetic promise of ruling authority, suggesting that those who remain faithful will share in Jesus' future reign (Psalm 2:8-9).

- "And I will give him the morning star." (Revelation 2:28)

- Morning Star: Often symbolizing Jesus Himself (Revelation 22:16), the morning star signifies hope, guidance, and the ultimate reward of eternal life in fellowship with Christ.

Application for Today: The Importance of Doctrinal Purity

The message to Thyatira has significant relevance to the modern church. Like Thyatira, today's church often grapples with the balance between love, good works, and doctrinal purity. While God values compassion and service, He also calls His people to remain steadfast against teachings that dilute or corrupt His truth. The warnings given to Thyatira emphasize the necessity of resisting false teachings, particularly those that encourage moral compromise and idolatry.

1. Discernment in Doctrine: Just as Thyatira was warned against false prophecy, the church today must discern true doctrine. False teachings that disguise themselves as "new truths" or progressive interpretations can lead believers away from biblical principles.

2. Tolerance vs. Compromise: While tolerance is often valued in Christian circles, there are limits when it comes to foundational truths. The church must resist the temptation to embrace cultural or secular ideologies that conflict with biblical teachings.

3. The Significance of Purity: Jesus' warning to Thyatira highlights the necessity of doctrinal and moral purity within the church. Love and good works are essential, but they must be undergirded by a commitment to sound doctrine.

4. The Call to Overcome: Jesus' promise to the overcomers reminds us that faithfulness to Him, even in the face of challenges, brings eternal rewards. The "morning star" symbolizes the ultimate hope and assurance for those who remain true to the gospel.

The church of Thyatira stands as both a caution and an encouragement to today's believers. While good works and growth in love are commendable, they must be anchored in unwavering commitment to God's truth.

Prophetic Significance of the Church of Thyatira

The church of Thyatira holds a profound prophetic significance, representing the dangers of compromise and the rise of false teachings within the body of Christ. In a prophetic sense, Thyatira reflects a period in church history and an enduring warning against tolerance of spiritual corruption. This message encourages churches today to prioritize doctrinal purity and resist influences that divert believers from Christ-centered faith and morality.

The Church of Thyatira as a Prophetic Symbol

1. Period of Spiritual Compromise (Middle Ages)

The church in Thyatira is often associated with a period in church history, particularly the Middle Ages, when doctrinal compromise became widespread. During this time, the institutional church grew in political power and worldly influence, often at the cost of spiritual purity and biblical truth. This era saw the rise of practices and teachings not grounded in Scripture, which distracted believers from a true relationship with God.

2. The Symbol of Jezebel: False Prophecy and Idolatry

The figure of "Jezebel" represents false prophecy, spiritual compromise, and the allure of idolatry. In the Old Testament, Jezebel led Israel into idol worship and immorality, and her symbolic presence in Thyatira illustrates the dangers of accommodating teachings that lead believers astray. This mirrors times in church history and in modern contexts where self-proclaimed "prophets" or teachers lead people away from the foundational truths of the Gospel.

3. Judgment and Reward

Jesus' warning to Thyatira underscores the consequences of tolerating false teachings and immoral practices. The promise of "great tribulation" to those who refuse to repent is a reminder of God's judgment on compromised spirituality, while the promise of authority and the "morning star" represents the ultimate reward for those who remain faithful. This dual message holds prophetic significance for both historical and contemporary churches.

How Thyatira Relates to the Church Today

1. Tolerance of False Teaching and Worldly Influence

Just as Thyatira tolerated Jezebel's influence, some churches today allow secular or pseudo-Christian teachings that conflict with biblical truth. The church's focus on outward appearances or growth can sometimes overshadow the importance of doctrinal integrity. The message to Thyatira encourages believers to reject influences that compromise their faith, urging vigilance in upholding scriptural principles even when societal or internal pressures encourage otherwise.

2. Warning Against Spiritual Compromise

In modern Christianity, the allure of materialism, self-help philosophies, and secular ideologies can easily infiltrate the church, mirroring the spirit of Jezebel. The church today must guard against teachings that prioritize earthly success over spiritual truth, distorting the Gospel to fit popular or cultural trends. Thyatira's message urges believers to pursue holiness, ensuring their works and worship align with God's standards.

3. Call for Repentance and Return to Purity

Just as Jesus extended a period for Jezebel and her followers to repent, the prophetic message of Thyatira calls today's church to turn away from spiritual compromise and rediscover a foundation rooted in Christ alone. This is a call for leaders and members to examine their beliefs and practices, seeking alignment with the true Gospel and repenting where they have fallen short.

4. Encouragement for the Faithful Remnant

For those who resist these corrupting influences, Thyatira's prophetic message is one of encouragement. Jesus promises that those who remain steadfast will be given "authority over the nations" and the "morning star" (Revelation 2:26-28). This promise reminds us that faithfulness to Christ, even when it involves rejecting popular teachings or practices, is rewarded in His Kingdom.

The prophetic significance of Thyatira's message is a reminder that the church must prioritize doctrinal purity, spiritual integrity, and unwavering faith in Christ's teachings. By rejecting false teachings and remaining committed to God's truth, believers align themselves with Christ's eternal promises and avoid the consequences of compromise. Thyatira's message calls the church today to stand firm against spiritual corruption, grounding its faith and works in God's

Word and preparing itself for the ultimate reward in Christ's Kingdom.

CHAPTER 05

SARDIS – THE DEAD CHURCH

Scripture Reference: Revelation 3:1-6

Introduction to the Church at Sardis

The church in Sardis represents a warning about the dangers of spiritual complacency. Although it appeared to be a thriving congregation, Jesus described it as dead, spiritually stagnant, and complacent. This church had a reputation for being alive, yet, in Christ's eyes, it was void of the vital signs of true, Spirit-led life. Jesus' message to Sardis highlights the importance of continual spiritual growth, authentic devotion, and vigilance against becoming complacent.

Historical Context of Sardis

Sardis was once a wealthy and important city in Asia Minor, known for its opulence and rich history. It had a reputation for being impregnable because of its location on a high, defensible plateau. However, over time, Sardis fell to conquerors due to negligence and a lack of vigilance, which serves as a fitting backdrop for Jesus' rebuke of the church's spiritual negligence. The church had a false sense of security, much like the city itself, and failed to remain spiritually alert and vibrant.

Exegesis and Commentary

1. Revelation 3:1 - "I know thy works, that thou hast a name that thou livest, and art dead."

In this opening verse, Jesus confronts Sardis with a harsh but honest assessment. The phrase "I know thy works" (G2041, ergon) refers to their deeds, indicating that Christ is fully aware of the activities of this church. However, these works are empty, devoid of true spiritual life. Despite having a "name" (G3686, onoma), or reputation, for being a living church, Jesus declares it "dead" (G3498, nekros), symbolizing its spiritual decay.

- Application of Strong's Concordance: The term nekros is associated with death or lifelessness, indicating that the church's vitality had ceased. This can represent a warning against relying on past achievements or reputation rather than cultivating a living, dynamic faith.

2. Revelation 3:2 - "Be watchful, and strengthen the things which remain, that are ready to die: for I have not found thy works perfect before God."

Here, Jesus urges the church to "be watchful" (G1127, gregoreo), meaning to be vigilant and alert. This word choice signifies the necessity of actively guarding one's spiritual life and not falling into complacency. The command to "strengthen" (G4741, sterizo) suggests that Sardis still has a remnant of faith, but it is fragile and must be reinforced.

- Commentary: This verse emphasizes that while Sardis was spiritually dead, there were still elements of faith and life remaining that could be revived. The phrase "I have not found thy works perfect" (G4137, pleroo) conveys that their deeds were incomplete and lacking in spiritual depth and authenticity. It's a call to pursue a fullness in their relationship with God.

3. Revelation 3:3 - "Remember therefore how thou hast received and heard, and hold fast, and repent. If therefore thou shalt not watch, I will come on thee as a thief, and thou shalt not know what hour I will come upon thee."

Jesus commands Sardis to "remember" (G3421, mnemoneuo) their original teachings and return to the roots of their faith. "Hold fast" (G2902, krateo) implies a call to grasp firmly onto these foundational truths, while "repent" (G3340, metanoeo) indicates a need for a heartfelt change of direction. The imagery of coming "as a thief" (G2812, kleptes) conveys suddenness and unexpected judgment.

- Prophetic Meaning: The thief analogy suggests that complacency leaves the church vulnerable to spiritual judgment. This is a call for vigilance, as spiritual lethargy can lead to severe consequences. The verse also reflects Jesus' emphasis on the urgency of repentance to avoid judgment.

4. Revelation 3:4 - "Thou hast a few names even in Sardis which have not defiled their garments; and they shall walk with me in white: for they are worthy."

In contrast to the overall lifelessness of the church, there are still "a few names" (G3686, onoma), faithful believers who have "not defiled their garments" (G3435, moluno), which suggests that they have maintained purity and devotion. The promise of walking "in white" (G3022, leukos) symbolizes purity, victory, and honor.

- Application: The remnant who remain pure represent hope within the church, demonstrating that personal integrity and holiness are possible even in a spiritually stagnant environment. They are deemed "worthy" (G514, axios), showing that true worthiness is tied to faithfulness and spiritual purity.

5. Revelation 3:5 - "He that overcometh, the same shall be clothed in white raiment; and I will not blot out his

name out of the book of life, but I will confess his name before my Father, and before his angels."

To the "overcomer" (G3528, nikao), Jesus promises eternal rewards. Being "clothed in white raiment" reflects purity and honor. The assurance of not blotting their names out of the "book of life" (G976, biblion of zoe) signifies eternal security for the faithful. Jesus also promises to "confess" (G3670, homologeo) their name before the Father, a profound affirmation of their faithfulness.

- Interpretation: This verse assures believers of their eternal place in God's presence, providing both encouragement and motivation to overcome spiritual complacency. The promise of Jesus advocating for them before God is a powerful testament to the importance of maintaining faithfulness.

6. Revelation 3:6 - "He that hath an ear, let him hear what the Spirit saith unto the churches."

This familiar refrain emphasizes the importance of paying attention to the Spirit's guidance. It's a call to not only hear but to respond to the message, applying it personally and collectively.

- Prophetic Insight: This message applies not just to Sardis, but to all believers. The Spirit's call is timeless, urging each generation to heed the warnings and encouragements Jesus provides to these churches.

Prophetic Significance of the Church of Sardis

The church of Sardis represents the perils of spiritual lethargy and the danger of having an outward appearance of vitality while lacking a genuine, life-giving connection to Christ. In a prophetic sense, Sardis could be seen as a warning to churches that appear active yet are spiritually hollow, calling them back to a vibrant relationship with God.

Application for Today's Church

The message to Sardis is especially relevant in today's context, where it's easy to become comfortable with religious rituals or social reputation without a dynamic spiritual life. Many churches and believers might be lulled into complacency, appearing outwardly faithful but lacking genuine intimacy with God.

1. Avoiding Complacency

Sardis' warning calls the church to continually renew its devotion, seek the Spirit's guidance, and pursue growth in Christ rather than relying on past successes.

2. Guarding Against Spiritual Stagnation

Just as Sardis needed to "strengthen what remains," churches today should emphasize discipleship, community, and spiritual accountability to nurture genuine faith.

3. Hope for the Faithful Remnant

Sardis reminds us that even in spiritually struggling environments, faithful believers can stand firm. This passage encourages those who remain faithful amidst widespread complacency, assuring them of God's recognition and eternal reward.

The message to the church in Sardis serves as a reminder that spiritual vitality cannot be replaced by reputation or external works. True faith is living, growing, and deeply connected to Christ. Sardis calls every believer to examine their faith honestly, strengthen their spiritual commitment, and live each day with renewed dedication to God's Word. Only through genuine, Spirit-led lives can believers fulfill the calling to be lights in a world that needs the transformative power of Christ.

The church at Sardis presents a powerful warning about the dangers of spiritual stagnation and complacency.

Though it had a reputation for being alive, Jesus' diagnosis of Sardis was blunt: it was spiritually dead. Despite the church's external appearance, Jesus called for a revival—a wake-up call that would shake the church out of its lethargy and bring it back to life. In this chapter, we explore the historical, spiritual, and prophetic aspects of this message, examining how it applies both to the church and individual believers today.

Historical Context of Sardis

Sardis was one of the wealthiest and most influential cities in Asia Minor, known for its luxurious lifestyle and rich heritage. Once considered nearly impregnable, the city had fallen twice due to negligence and overconfidence. This backdrop is significant, as it parallels the church's own condition of spiritual overconfidence and neglect. Sardis had a long-standing reputation as a powerful city, yet its history of invasions due to a lack of vigilance foreshadows the spiritual issues within the church.

Exegesis and Commentary

1. Revelation 3:1 - "And unto the angel of the church in Sardis write; These things saith he that hath the seven Spirits of God, and the seven stars; I know thy works, that thou hast a name that thou livest, and art dead."

In this verse, Jesus introduces Himself as the One with the "seven Spirits of God" (G4151, pneuma), representing the fullness of the Holy Spirit, and the "seven stars" (G792, aster), symbolizing His authority over the churches. He declares, "I know thy works" (G2041, ergon), exposing the reality behind their reputation. Despite their name for being "alive" (G2198, zao), Jesus pronounces them "dead" (G3498, nekros).

- Application of Strong's Concordance: The Greek word nekros (G3498) signifies lifelessness, underlining the church's profound spiritual decay. Sardis' reputation did not match its true state, serving as a reminder that outward appearances and activity are not always signs of spiritual health.

- Spiritual Insight: This verse warns against the dangers of self-deception, where one's faith life may appear active but is actually devoid of the Spirit's transformative power. Sardis' lack of spiritual vibrancy is a call for Christians to seek authentic encounters with God and to live in alignment with His Spirit.

2. Revelation 3:2 - "Be watchful, and strengthen the things which remain, that are ready to die: for I have not found thy works perfect before God."

Jesus' command to "be watchful" (G1127, gregoreo) implies vigilance and spiritual alertness, suggesting that Sardis had become lethargic and inattentive to spiritual matters. "Strengthen" (G4741, sterizo) means to reinforce or support, indicating that while most of the church was dead, there were aspects that could still be revived.

- Interpretation: Jesus emphasizes the need for proactive measures to strengthen faith. "Perfect" (G4137, pleroo) in this context means complete or fulfilled, revealing that the church's works were incomplete in God's eyes. This underscores that good works should be rooted in genuine devotion rather than mere routine.

- Practical Application: This verse urges believers to examine their spiritual condition regularly and to fortify any aspects of their faith that may be weakening. It's a call to cultivate a vibrant relationship with God and to ensure that one's works reflect a heart of love and obedience to Him.

3. Revelation 3:3 - "Remember therefore how thou hast received and heard, and hold fast, and repent. If therefore thou shalt not watch, I will come on thee as a thief, and thou shalt not know what hour I will come upon thee."

Jesus urges Sardis to "remember" (G3421, mnemoneuo) the gospel teachings they once "received" (G3880, paralambano) and "heard" (G191, akouo). He commands them to "hold fast" (G2902, krateo) to these truths and to "repent" (G3340, metanoeo), calling for a sincere return to their initial zeal and purity of faith.

- Prophetic Warning: The metaphor of Jesus coming "as a thief" (G2812, kleptes) conveys sudden judgment. This imagery emphasizes the importance of being spiritually alert, as the timing of His judgment will be unexpected for those who are spiritually unprepared.

- Contemporary Relevance: This passage stresses the need for believers to guard their faith actively and to remember foundational gospel truths. The call to repentance is a reminder that no matter how far one may drift, restoration is always possible through turning back to Christ.

4. Revelation 3:4 - "Thou hast a few names even in Sardis which have not defiled their garments; and they shall walk with me in white: for they are worthy."

In this verse, Jesus acknowledges a faithful remnant in Sardis who have "not defiled" (G3435, moluno) their garments, a symbol of purity and righteousness. The promise to "walk with me in white" (G3022, leukos) signifies the honor, purity, and eternal fellowship with Christ awaiting the faithful.

- Insight from Strong's: Leukos (G3022) indicates whiteness, symbolizing purity, victory, and sanctity. Jesus' acknowledgment of a remnant shows that, even within a spiritually decaying church, there are those who remain faithful.

- Application: This message assures believers that even in compromising or spiritually dead environments, individuals can maintain their commitment to purity. Christ values this integrity and promises eternal companionship for those who remain steadfast.

5. Revelation 3:5 - "He that overcometh, the same shall be clothed in white raiment; and I will not blot out his

name out of the book of life, but I will confess his name before my Father, and before his angels."

To "overcome" (G3528, nikao) is a call to conquer or triumph spiritually. The promise of being "clothed in white raiment" (G3022, leukos) signifies the ultimate victory over spiritual death. Jesus' assurance that their names will remain in the "book of life" (G976, biblion of zoe) speaks to their eternal security.

- Prophetic Assurance: The promise of eternal life is for those who persevere in faith, despite challenges or spiritual decay around them. Jesus' confession before the Father reflects His advocacy for faithful believers, ensuring their place in the kingdom.

6. Revelation 3:6 - "He that hath an ear, let him hear what the Spirit saith unto the churches."

This final exhortation highlights the importance of attentiveness to the Spirit's message. It's an invitation to every believer to listen and respond to the Spirit's call for revival, transformation, and renewed faith.

- Practical Reflection: This call is timeless, urging churches and believers to remain sensitive to the Spirit's leading, heed the warnings, and pursue a life of authentic faith.

Prophetic Meaning and Application for Today's Church

The church at Sardis symbolizes the perils of spiritual complacency, a caution against relying on reputation and external activity without true inward devotion. Sardis' spiritual deadness warns today's churches about the risks of prioritizing appearance over genuine faith.

1. Spiritual Revival as a Priority

Jesus' call to "wake up" in Sardis is a profound call for revival. Many modern churches can appear vibrant externally but lack the internal life of the Spirit. Sardis reminds churches to renew their focus on prayer, discipleship, and a true relationship with God.

2. Guarding Against Complacency

Sardis' warning underscores the need for churches and believers to remain vigilant. Overconfidence in past achievements or appearances can lead to a state of spiritual dormancy. Churches are encouraged to evaluate their practices continually, ensuring they reflect a commitment to Christ.

3. Promise for the Faithful Remnant

Sardis serves as a reminder that, even in spiritually challenging environments, faithful individuals can stand firm. The promise of eternal reward and fellowship with Christ is for those who overcome, staying true to their faith despite surrounding spiritual apathy.

The message to the church in Sardis calls each believer to evaluate the state of their faith. Are we relying on appearance, reputation, or past successes? Or are we actively pursuing a living relationship with Christ? Jesus' words to Sardis are a powerful reminder to "wake up" and return to the vitality of Spirit-led life.

Prophetic Significance of Sardis—The Dead Church

The church of Sardis, with its spiritually dead condition despite an appearance of vitality, serves as a prophetic symbol for the dangers of complacency and spiritual stagnation in the church across generations. It reflects a period in church history where external observances and reputations overshadowed genuine spiritual life and commitment. This prophetic insight holds profound implications for the church today, emphasizing the need for revival, sincere faith, and authenticity.

Historical-Prophetic Interpretation

The church at Sardis is often associated with the Reformation period in church history, approximately from the 16th to the 18th centuries. During this time, many churches became steeped in rituals, traditions, and outward appearances of spirituality, often without a deep personal relationship with God or true spiritual vitality. While the Reformation addressed critical doctrinal issues and returned certain teachings to a biblical foundation, some denominations still leaned heavily on formality, establishing reputations without fostering genuine, life-changing faith within the hearts of their members.

The Prophetic Warnings and Messages for Today

1. Appearance without Substance

- Just as Sardis was known for being "alive" in name but was pronounced "dead" by Jesus, many churches today may seem vibrant on the outside, with impressive programs, activities, and even doctrinal correctness, yet lack the Holy Spirit's true transforming power. This prophetic message calls the church to assess not only its outward appearance but also its inward spiritual health.

2. The Call to "Wake Up"

- The command to "wake up" (Revelation 3:2) signifies a call for spiritual alertness and revival, not just for Sardis but also for today's church. Jesus' message to Sardis is a reminder to revive the faith that once burned brightly but has since grown cold or routine. The church today is called to awaken from any spiritual lethargy, pursue God with renewed fervor, and actively engage in heartfelt worship and service.

3. Retaining a Faithful Remnant

- Jesus' acknowledgment of the few faithful individuals in Sardis ("a few names even in Sardis which have not defiled their garments," Revelation 3:4) highlights the enduring presence of a faithful remnant in any church, regardless of its general condition. This remnant serves as a prophetic assurance that even when a church may seem largely compromised or spiritually inactive, there are always individuals within it who remain deeply committed to God. These people are the catalysts for revival and the examples for others to follow.

4. Overcoming and Eternal Rewards

- Jesus' promise of white garments and a secure place in the "book of life" for those who "overcome" (Revelation 3:5) is a powerful prophetic reminder of the eternal rewards awaiting those who persevere in faith. In today's context, this message serves as an encouragement for believers to stand firm, even when surrounded by complacency or spiritual decay. Those who remain faithful will receive not only the "crown of life" but also a permanent, unshakable place in God's kingdom.

Application to Modern Christian Life and Church

The church of Sardis represents a cautionary tale for contemporary Christians, showing that spiritual complacency can easily set in, especially when religious activity becomes a substitute for a true relationship with Christ. The message to Sardis urges believers today to examine their faith life and resist the tendency to rely on past successes or reputations, instead pursuing a dynamic, personal connection with God.

In modern application, the church of Sardis warns against becoming "spiritually dead" while appearing outwardly active. It calls churches and individuals to:

- Self-Examination: Regularly assess their true spiritual state, examining if their works are rooted in love for God or merely habitual.

- Seek Revival: Actively pursue spiritual renewal, emphasizing the importance of the Holy Spirit and prayer in revitalizing one's faith and community.

- Stay Alert: Be vigilant against spiritual complacency and be willing to repent and return to foundational gospel truths if they have drifted.

- Embrace Holiness: Commit to purity and integrity, embodying a life that is in alignment with God's will, even in a world that encourages compromise.

Sardis and the Call for Authentic Faith

The church at Sardis symbolizes the risks associated with a faith that is superficial and lacking in true life. Its prophetic significance urges the church today to "wake up," to guard against the drift toward spiritual routine, and to reignite a passion for God that goes beyond mere appearance.

Jesus' call to Sardis is a call for all believers to seek the fullness of the Holy Spirit and to live lives marked by authenticity, commitment, and the transformative power of God.

CHAPTER 06

PHILADELPHIA – THE FAITHFUL CHURCH

Scripture Reference: Revelation 3:7-13

Condition of Philadelphia:

Philadelphia, known as the "Faithful Church," receives only praise from Jesus, with no rebuke. This church remained steadfast in its works and loyalty to Christ despite its challenges. Jesus commended their perseverance and rewarded their faithfulness by granting them open doors of opportunity and a promise of protection.

Background and Historical Context

The city of Philadelphia, located in Asia Minor (modern-day Turkey), was established as a missionary city with a purpose of spreading Greek culture and language. Known as "the city of brotherly love," Philadelphia had fertile lands, but it was prone to earthquakes. Despite its susceptibility to natural disasters, the church there held fast to its faith. This church represents spiritual resilience, even with limited power, and it demonstrates that genuine faithfulness can open doors to powerful opportunities and blessings.

Verse-by-Verse Analysis and Commentary

Revelation 3:7

> "And to the angel of the church in Philadelphia write: These things saith he that is holy, he that is true, he that hath the key of David, he that openeth, and no man shutteth; and shutteth, and no man openeth."

Strong's Concordance Analysis

- Holy (Greek: hagios, Strong's G40): Sacred, morally blameless, separated unto God.

- True (Greek: alēthinos, Strong's G228): Real, genuine, sincere, opposed to what is false.

- Key of David (Greek: kleis Dauid, Strong's G2807 & G1138): Symbolic of authority and power, specifically in opening or closing access.

Commentary

Jesus introduces Himself to the church in Philadelphia as "holy" and "true." These qualities reflect His sinless nature and unchanging character, highlighting that He is completely trustworthy. The "key of David" signifies His authority over the Kingdom of God, symbolizing the power to open doors (opportunities, revelations, and salvation) that no one else can close. This statement emphasizes that Jesus alone has sovereign control over His church, and His decisions cannot be overridden by any human or spiritual power.

Revelation 3:8

> "I know thy works: behold, I have set before thee an open door, and no man can shut it: for thou hast a little strength, and hast kept my word, and hast not denied my name."

Strong's Concordance Analysis

- Open door (Greek: thura anoigō, Strong's G2374 & G455): A metaphor for new opportunities or access, often used in the context of evangelism and the spread of the gospel.

- Little strength (Greek: mikros dunamis, Strong's G3398 & G1411): Indicating that their strength was limited, but sufficient through their reliance on God.

Commentary

Jesus acknowledges the works of the Philadelphia church and presents them with an "open door." This can be seen as an opportunity for mission work and spiritual growth. Their "little strength" suggests that although they might not have been large or powerful by worldly standards, their faithfulness made them spiritually resilient. This church's unwavering loyalty, obedience to Jesus' teachings, and refusal to deny His name stand as models of steadfast commitment, showing that spiritual strength lies in faithfulness rather than size or influence.

Revelation 3:9

> "Behold, I will make them of the synagogue of Satan, which say they are Jews, and are not, but do lie; behold, I will make them to come and worship before thy feet, and to know that I have loved thee."

Strong's Concordance Analysis

- Synagogue of Satan (Greek: synagōgē Satanas, Strong's G4864 & G4567): Refers to those who oppose the true believers and the gospel.

- Worship before thy feet (Greek: proskuneō enopion ho pous sou, Strong's G4352 & G1799 & G4228): An act of acknowledgment and submission.

Commentary

Here, Jesus refers to those who falsely claim to be His followers but actively oppose the true church. Jesus assures the church that He will vindicate them, causing their persecutors to recognize the authenticity of their faith. This image underscores that true followers of Christ will be vindicated, and God will reveal His love for them even in the face of opposition.

Revelation 3:10

> "Because thou hast kept the word of my patience, I also will keep thee from the hour of temptation, which shall come upon all the world, to try them that dwell upon the earth."

Strong's Concordance Analysis

- Word of my patience (Greek: logos ho hupomonē mou, Strong's G3056 & G5281): The message of endurance, highlighting their adherence to Christ's call to persevere.

- Hour of temptation (Greek: hōra peirasmos, Strong's G5610 & G3986): A period of trial or testing.

Commentary

The church at Philadelphia receives a promise of protection because they have remained patient and endured trials. The "hour of temptation" may refer to a specific period of testing for the whole earth. Christ's assurance that He will "keep" them from this period can be understood as protection or even exemption from trials. This promise encourages believers to endure, confident in God's faithfulness to protect His people.

Revelation 3:11

> "Behold, I come quickly: hold that fast which thou hast, that no man take thy crown."

Strong's Concordance Analysis

- Come quickly (Greek: erchomai tachu, Strong's G2064 & G5035): An urgent promise of Christ's imminent return.

- Crown (Greek: stephanos, Strong's G4735): Symbolic of victory and reward.

Commentary

Jesus' assurance of His soon return urges the believers to "hold fast" to their faith so that they may not lose their "crown"—a reward for enduring faith. This admonition is a reminder that steadfastness is necessary even for the faithful, as spiritual rewards await those who endure until the end.

Revelation 3:12-13

> "Him that overcometh will I make a pillar in the temple of my God, and he shall go no more out: and I will write upon him the name of my God, and the name of the city of my God, which is new Jerusalem, which cometh down out of heaven from my God: and I will write upon him my new name. He that hath an ear, let him hear what the Spirit saith unto the churches."

Strong's Concordance Analysis

- Pillar (Greek: stulos, Strong's G4769): Symbol of stability and permanence.

- Name of my God, new Jerusalem, my new name (Greek: onoma ho theos mou, kainos Ierousalēm, kainos onoma mou, Strong's G3686 & G2316 & G2419 & G2537): Indicating identity, ownership, and belonging to God.

Commentary

The promise to make the overcomer a "pillar" signifies permanence and security within God's eternal kingdom. Writing the names of God, the New Jerusalem, and Jesus' "new name" on the believer indicates divine ownership and everlasting fellowship. This profound promise assures believers that their faithfulness will be rewarded with eternal security and belonging in God's kingdom.

Application for Today

The message to Philadelphia challenges today's church to remain steadfast, even when resources or influence seem limited. Christ's recognition of their "little strength" but unwavering faithfulness encourages believers that genuine commitment to God's Word, regardless of external power, opens doors of opportunity. It highlights that Jesus values faithfulness over worldly status and that steadfastness will be rewarded with protection, security, and eternal fellowship in God's kingdom.

Prophetic Meaning of Philadelphia in Today's Life

The church in Philadelphia prophetically represents an era of missionary zeal and perseverance in the face of hardship. Today, it symbolizes churches that may seem small or marginalized but are rich in faith and commitment. The church at Philadelphia reminds Christians of the power of unwavering dedication to God's Word and the promise of open doors, protection, and eternal reward for those who remain faithful to Christ.

The Prophetic Significance of the Church in Philadelphia

Revelation 3:7-13: Philadelphia as a Symbol of the Faithful Church

The church in Philadelphia prophetically represents the faithful believers throughout history, and especially in the era before the final apostasy, often associated with the church in Laodicea. Philadelphia's faithfulness, resilience, and refusal to compromise align with a remnant of believers who remain loyal to God's Word and Christ, despite challenges and societal pressures. The "open door" of opportunity given to Philadelphia has often been interpreted as symbolic of the missionary movement and evangelistic efforts, through which the gospel has spread to the world.

Prophetic Significance and How It Relates to the Church Today

The church in Philadelphia exemplifies the model of a faithful, enduring church that stands firm in its beliefs and mission. In today's context, it represents the part of the global church that continues to prioritize obedience to God, spreading the gospel, and showing unwavering loyalty to Christ, regardless of opposition or difficulties.

Verse-by-Verse Prophetic Analysis and Commentary

Revelation 3:7 - The Authority of Christ Over the Church

> "And to the angel of the church in Philadelphia write: These things saith he that is holy, he that is true, he that hath the key of David, he that openeth, and no man shutteth; and shutteth, and no man openeth."

Strong's Concordance Analysis

- Key of David (Greek: kleis Dauid, Strong's G2807 & G1138): Symbolizes the authority of Christ to open or close doors to the Kingdom, aligning with prophecy in Isaiah 22:22 about God's ultimate control over His kingdom.

Prophetic Commentary

The reference to the "key of David" highlights Christ's supreme authority over the church, both historically and prophetically. In the present age, this authority signifies that Christ alone opens the way for spiritual opportunities, mission work, and advancement of the gospel. For believers today, this is a call to trust in Christ's power to open doors, even in places where access seems limited or obstructed.

Revelation 3:8 - The Open Door of Evangelism and Spiritual Growth

> "I know thy works: behold, I have set before thee an open door, and no man can shut it: for thou hast a little strength, and hast kept my word, and hast not denied my name."

Strong's Concordance Analysis

- Open door (Greek: thura anoigō, Strong's G2374 & G455): Symbolizes access, often understood as evangelistic or spiritual opportunities.

Prophetic Commentary

The "open door" can be seen prophetically as a period in church history marked by widespread evangelism and missionary expansion. In modern times, this speaks to the church's calling to spread the gospel globally, leveraging any opportunity provided. Despite facing persecution or challenges, faithful churches have maintained their mission, seeing God's power work through them. Today, believers are encouraged to remain steadfast and continue spreading Christ's message, even with limited resources.

Revelation 3:9 - Vindication of the Faithful

> "Behold, I will make them of the synagogue of Satan, which say they are Jews, and are not, but do lie; behold, I will make them to come and worship before thy feet, and to know that I have loved thee."

Strong's Concordance Analysis

- Synagogue of Satan (Greek: synagōgē Satanas, Strong's G4864 & G4567): Refers to opposition forces that masquerade as religious yet contradict the gospel truth.

Prophetic Commentary

Jesus' promise to make the false opposition acknowledge the truth serves as both encouragement and prophecy for the faithful. Historically, faithful Christians have faced opposition from those who distort the truth. In today's context, this assurance promises that the church will ultimately be vindicated, and the faithfulness of genuine believers will be revealed. This passage reminds the modern church that faithfulness will be recognized, even by those who opposed or misunderstood their mission.

Revelation 3:10 - Promise of Protection

> "Because thou hast kept the word of my patience, I also will keep thee from the hour of temptation, which shall come upon all the world, to try them that dwell upon the earth."

Strong's Concordance Analysis

- Hour of temptation (Greek: hōra peirasmos, Strong's G5610 & G3986): A specific time of testing, often interpreted as a period of tribulation or trial.

Prophetic Commentary

The "hour of temptation" can be viewed as a prophetic reference to times of testing and persecution that would come upon the world, which some interpret as referring to a future tribulation. For the faithful, this assurance signifies God's protective care, whether through deliverance from or perseverance in trials. Today, this promise serves to remind believers of God's sovereignty in times of global challenges and the certainty of divine protection for those who remain steadfast.

Revelation 3:11 - Holding Fast to the Faith

> "Behold, I come quickly: hold that fast which thou hast, that no man take thy crown."

Strong's Concordance Analysis

- Come quickly (Greek: erchomai tachu, Strong's G2064 & G5035): Implies urgency and the certainty of Christ's return.

- Crown (Greek: stephanos, Strong's G4735): Symbolizes victory, reward for enduring faith.

Prophetic Commentary

The exhortation to "hold fast" is particularly significant in a prophetic sense, as it speaks to the endurance required of believers before Christ's return. In today's context, this verse encourages the church to remain faithful, guarding against compromise and holding firmly to the truths of the gospel. It serves as a call for vigilance and resilience, with a promise of eternal reward for those who persevere.

Revelation 3:12-13 - Eternal Rewards for the Faithful

> "Him that overcometh will I make a pillar in the temple of my God, and he shall go no more out: and I will write upon him the name of my God, and the name of the city of my God, which is new Jerusalem, which cometh down out of heaven from my God: and I will write upon him my new name."

Strong's Concordance Analysis

- Pillar (Greek: stulos, Strong's G4769): Represents stability, support, and permanence within God's presence.

- Name of my God (Greek: onoma ho theos mou, Strong's G3686): Signifies belonging, ownership, and intimate relationship with God.

Prophetic Commentary

The promise to be made a "pillar" in God's temple conveys the ultimate reward for the faithful. Prophetically, this represents eternal security and a permanent place in God's presence. The "new name" written upon believers speaks to their transformed identity in Christ. For the church today, this serves as a powerful reminder that faithfulness leads to a deep, lasting relationship with God, symbolizing an unbreakable bond and a promise of eternal life.

Application for Today

In many ways, Philadelphia stands as an example for the church today to model its commitment, loyalty, and unwavering faithfulness to the truth of the gospel. In a world with competing ideologies, temptations, and pressures to conform, the church in Philadelphia is a prophetic symbol of strength and encouragement for modern believers.

1. Faithful Evangelism - The "open door" provided to Philadelphia calls the church to pursue evangelistic efforts, reaching out with the gospel to a world in need. It's a reminder to be active in mission work and make use of the spiritual opportunities that God provides.

2. Steadfast Endurance - The commendation for keeping God's Word with "little strength" encourages believers today to persevere even when resources seem scarce. Spiritual power is not measured in numbers or influence but in faithfulness.

3. Rejection of Compromise - Philadelphia remained loyal to Christ's name, refusing to compromise. This highlights the importance of doctrinal purity and resistance against false teachings.

4. Promise of Eternal Security - The reward of being a "pillar" assures believers that their faithfulness will result in eternal belonging with God, a promise of stability, protection, and a permanent place in His presence.

The prophetic message of Philadelphia calls the church today to remain faithful to its core mission, grounded in love, truth, and the unshakable authority of Christ. This church embodies the virtues of resilience, commitment, and spiritual openness that lead to God's favor and eternal reward. In times of trials and tribulations, the church can draw hope from Philadelphia's example, holding fast to the promises of God, knowing that the rewards for faithfulness are both immediate and everlasting.

Philadelphia—Application for Today: The Faithful Church

Introduction

The message to the church at Philadelphia holds a timeless lesson: faithfulness, despite limited strength or influence, opens doors for God's purpose to unfold. Today's churches can draw valuable insights from Philadelphia's example of perseverance, humility, and unwavering devotion to Christ, leading to unique blessings and ministry opportunities. By using expository study, we can delve into the depth of this message, exploring the historical context, scriptural insights, and spiritual applications for contemporary believers.

1. Remaining Faithful in All Circumstances (Revelation 3:8)

In Revelation 3:8, Jesus says, "I know thy works: behold, I have set before thee an open door, and no man can shut it: for thou hast a little strength, and hast kept my word, and hast not denied my name." Here, "works" (Greek: ergon, Strong's G2041) signifies not only actions but the faithfulness that motivates them. Jesus acknowledges Philadelphia's unwavering commitment, underscoring that even with limited strength (dynamis, Strong's G1411), their perseverance in keeping His word led to divine recognition and favor.

Application: Faithfulness, Not Power

This verse teaches that God honors consistency in holding to the truth of His word, regardless of influence or worldly power. The church in Philadelphia was likely small, having "little strength," yet their faithfulness allowed God to use them mightily. Today, churches with limited resources or members may feel inadequate, but this message confirms that God values commitment over size. His favor is on those who stay true to His name.

Open Door of Opportunity

The "open door" (Greek: thura, Strong's G2374) here represents not only protection but opportunities for ministry, service, and evangelism. In today's context, this open door speaks to the opportunities God provides for faithful churches to impact their communities and even the world. Churches today can trust that their faithfulness will lead to divine opportunities that "no man can shut," recognizing that these moments to spread the gospel and influence others are God-ordained and sustained.

2. Overcoming Opposition and Persecution (Revelation 3:9)

In Revelation 3:9, Jesus assures the Philadelphian church of His vindication: "Behold, I will make them of the synagogue of Satan, which say they are Jews, and are not, but do lie; behold, I will make them to come and worship before thy feet, and to know that I have loved thee." The "synagogue of Satan" (Greek: synagoge tou Satana, Strong's G4864, G4567) refers to those who opposed and undermined the faith of true believers.

Application: Standing Strong Against Cultural Pressures

This verse is relevant to today's churches, which may face opposition or cultural pressures that challenge their beliefs. Just as Philadelphia's faithfulness was tested, contemporary churches encounter ideologies and societal pressures that tempt them to compromise. However, God promises that those who remain steadfast will ultimately witness the truth prevail. The reminder that Christ's love sustains His people is a call for modern churches to persevere, knowing they are validated by God Himself.

3. Assurance of Protection and Deliverance (Revelation 3:10)

In Revelation 3:10, Jesus says, "Because thou hast kept the word of my patience, I also will keep thee from the hour of temptation, which shall come upon all the world, to try them that dwell upon the earth." Here, "kept" (Greek: tereo, Strong's G5083) denotes guarding or preserving, highlighting the church's diligent adherence to Christ's teachings. The "hour of temptation" (Greek: hora tou peirasmou, Strong's G5610, G3986) is a period of trial that Christ assures He will shield them from.

Application: Divine Protection Amidst Trials

This promise resonates for today's church, reminding believers that God's protection is not the absence of trials but the assurance of His presence and strength within them. As they endure various trials—whether through persecution, spiritual testing, or challenges to their faith—churches can take comfort in knowing that God's sustaining power preserves them. Churches facing adversity are encouraged by this message to hold fast, confident that God will uphold them in times of testing.

4. Eternal Rewards for Faithfulness (Revelation 3:12)

In verse 12, Jesus promises, "Him that overcometh will I make a pillar in the temple of my God, and he shall go no more out." The term "pillar" (Greek: stulos, Strong's G4769) implies stability, strength, and permanence, attributes that signify honor and unshakable standing within God's eternal kingdom. This promise of being established as a pillar reflects not only stability but also eternal belonging.

Application: Embracing Our Eternal Security

For modern churches, this image of being made a pillar in God's temple signifies a lasting, honored place in His presence. Churches today are reminded that their faithfulness on earth has eternal implications. This call invites believers to view their service and commitment not as temporary acts but as contributions to an everlasting kingdom. The promise of God's name written on them (Revelation 3:12) signifies a deep relationship with Him, affirming their identity and purpose for eternity.

5. Staying Faithful in Weakness

The church in Philadelphia was characterized by its "little strength" but unwavering faith. This principle is powerfully relevant for churches today that may feel overshadowed or small compared to others. Philadelphia's example teaches that spiritual strength lies in reliance on God, not on numbers or resources. This perspective challenges churches to prioritize spiritual health and unity in Christ over external success or worldly influence.

Application: Encouragement for Small or Struggling Congregations

Small congregations often wonder if their impact is significant enough. Philadelphia's example proves that God sees and rewards faithfulness regardless of size. Every church, no matter its size or situation, can trust that God values their sincere devotion. This chapter reassures small or struggling churches that they are a vital part of God's plan, carrying His presence and power within them.

Summary and Reflection

Philadelphia stands as a timeless model of faithfulness for today's churches. They were commended not for their strength or size but for their commitment to Christ, showing that true faithfulness transcends physical resources. By remaining true to His word, rejecting compromise, and trusting in God's protection, Philadelphia became an example of a church that is spiritually alive, impactful, and eternally secure.

For contemporary churches, the message to Philadelphia encourages a return to genuine devotion, faithfulness, and endurance. Faithfulness, despite outward limitations, is God's criterion for success, inviting churches to deepen their dependence on Him. God's promise of an "open door" reassures believers today that spiritual commitment yields divine opportunities and eternal rewards, confirming that God is ever mindful of His faithful ones.

The church of Philadelphia encourages today's believers to remain steadfast, trusting that God honors genuine faithfulness over worldly success. In a world where churches often measure influence by size, wealth, or visibility, Philadelphia's legacy is a call to humility and endurance. The promise of an open door, protection in trials, and an eternal place as "pillars" in God's kingdom gives every church the hope and confidence to stand firm, knowing that their faithfulness has both present and eternal significance.

CHAPTER 07

LAODICEA – THE LUKEWARM CHURCH

The church at Laodicea, the final church addressed in Revelation, receives a stark rebuke. Unlike other churches, Laodicea is neither praised for any of its deeds nor encouraged in its state. Known for its material wealth and self-sufficiency, the church at Laodicea was spiritually destitute. Jesus warns them that their lukewarmness—neither "hot" nor "cold"—leaves Him with no choice but to "spew" them out of His mouth. Through an expository study of Revelation 3:14-22, we will explore Laodicea's spiritual state, Christ's call for repentance, and the relevance of this message for today's church.

1. Jesus' Address to Laodicea: The Amen and Faithful Witness (Revelation 3:14)

In Revelation 3:14, Jesus begins by saying, "These things saith the Amen, the faithful and true witness, the beginning of the creation of God." Here, "Amen" (Greek: amen, Strong's G281) is used as a title, signifying Jesus as the final, unchanging authority—His words are faithful and certain. As the "faithful and true witness" (Greek: pistos kai alethinos martys, Strong's G4103, G227, G3144), Jesus embodies ultimate truth and reliability.

Application: Recognizing Jesus as the Final Authority

This verse reminds believers that Jesus is both the beginning and the end, the one whose testimony and standards do not change. Today's churches, much like Laodicea, need to recognize Christ as the ultimate authority rather than relying on worldly status or wealth. By acknowledging Him as the faithful witness, churches today can measure their spiritual health according to His standards, not by outward appearances or success.

2. Spiritual Lukewarmness: Neither Hot nor Cold (Revelation 3:15-16)

In Revelation 3:15-16, Jesus addresses Laodicea's condition directly: "I know thy works, that thou art neither cold nor hot: I would thou wert cold or hot. So then because thou art lukewarm, and neither cold nor hot, I will spue thee out of my mouth." The term "lukewarm" (Greek: chliaros, Strong's G5513) here refers to a state of apathy or indifference, contrasting with the enthusiasm of being either "hot" (Greek: zestos, Strong's G2200) or "cold" (Greek: psychros, Strong's G5593).

Application: Avoiding Spiritual Apathy

This rebuke challenges churches and believers who have grown complacent in their faith. Lukewarmness often results from compromise, half-heartedness, or prioritizing material comforts over spiritual commitment. Today's church is warned against a superficial faith that is indifferent to the things of God. Instead, it is encouraged to embrace a fervent, passionate relationship with Christ, avoiding the "lukewarm" approach that provokes Christ's dissatisfaction.

3. Self-Sufficiency and Spiritual Poverty (Revelation 3:17)

In Revelation 3:17, Jesus describes Laodicea's self-perception and reality: "Because thou sayest, I am rich, and increased with goods, and have need of nothing; and knowest not that thou art wretched, and miserable, and poor, and blind, and naked." The church's self-reliance and material wealth led to spiritual pride and blindness. The terms "poor" (Greek: ptochos, Strong's G4434) and "blind" (Greek: typhlos, Strong's G5185) indicate a severe lack of spiritual insight, despite their material prosperity.

Application: Recognizing True Wealth in Christ

Many churches today are susceptible to the same pitfall, measuring success by finances, buildings, or social influence. However, Christ's assessment is that these do not define true wealth. Spiritual riches come from a relationship with Christ, not from worldly acquisitions. Churches and individuals must guard against the pride of self-sufficiency and recognize their dependence on God's grace for true spiritual wealth.

4. Christ's Counsel: Gold Refined in Fire and White Garments (Revelation 3:18)

In Revelation 3:18, Jesus advises the Laodiceans: "I counsel thee to buy of me gold tried in the fire, that thou mayest be rich; and white raiment, that thou mayest be clothed, and that the shame of thy nakedness do not appear; and anoint thine eyes with eyesalve, that thou mayest see." Here, "gold" (Greek: chrysion, Strong's G5557) refined by fire symbolizes faith and character purified through trials. "White raiment" (Greek: leukos himation, Strong's G3022, G2440) represents purity and righteousness.

Application: Seeking Spiritual Refinement and Purity

Christ's counsel is a call to seek spiritual richness over material wealth. "Gold tried in the fire" represents enduring faith developed through trials, while "white raiment" symbolizes purity that comes from living a righteous life. Churches are encouraged to prioritize spiritual transformation over external appearances, focusing on character, humility, and holiness as markers of true wealth in Christ. Applying this counsel, believers are called to pursue righteousness and reject compromise.

5. Repentance and Renewal (Revelation 3:19)

In Revelation 3:19, Jesus expresses His love through discipline: "As many as I love, I rebuke and chasten: be zealous therefore, and repent." The term "rebuke" (Greek: elegcho, Strong's G1651) refers to conviction of sin, and "chasten" (Greek: paideuo, Strong's G3811) implies correction. Jesus' call to repentance reveals His desire for restoration, not rejection.

Application: Embracing Christ's Loving Discipline

This verse encourages churches and believers to welcome correction as a sign of Christ's love. Spiritual apathy, like that seen in Laodicea, can only be overcome by a heart of repentance and a renewed zeal for God. Churches are urged to respond to Christ's rebuke by turning from complacency and reigniting their passion for Him, embracing discipline as a step toward restoration.

6. Christ's Invitation: Open the Door (Revelation 3:20)

One of the most well-known verses, Revelation 3:20, says, "Behold, I stand at the door, and knock: if any man hear my voice, and open the door, I will come in to him, and will sup with him, and he with me." Jesus' invitation to "open the door" (Greek: thyra, Strong's G2374) signifies a personal relationship and intimacy with Him.

Application: Inviting Christ into Daily Life

Christ's desire for a close, daily relationship with His followers is highlighted here. He patiently waits for an invitation, longing to share in fellowship. For believers and churches today, this verse serves as a reminder to keep the door open for Christ's presence and guidance in all aspects of life. Embracing this invitation deepens their walk with Him, replacing complacency with genuine devotion and intimacy.

7. Promise to the Overcomer (Revelation 3:21)

In Revelation 3:21, Jesus promises, "To him that overcometh will I grant to sit with me in my throne, even as I also overcame, and am set down with my Father in his throne." This promise emphasizes "overcoming" (Greek: nikao, Strong's G3528), the call to conquer complacency and pursue faithfulness.

Application: Pursuing Faithfulness and Victory in Christ

This promise offers encouragement to believers to remain faithful and to strive for victory in their spiritual lives. Just as Christ overcame, believers are called to overcome spiritual apathy and self-sufficiency. Churches today are urged to hold fast to their faith, finding strength in Christ's victory to overcome their struggles and be rewarded with eternal fellowship in His presence.

Summary and Reflection

Laodicea's spiritual condition serves as a profound warning against complacency, self-sufficiency, and superficial spirituality. Despite their material prosperity, their lukewarmness left them spiritually bankrupt, and Jesus' stern warning was a call to re-evaluate their priorities. In today's context, this message encourages churches to seek true spiritual riches by pursuing humility, repentance, and an intimate relationship with Christ.

The promise of communion with Christ is given to those who open the door to His presence. For the church today, Laodicea's story is a reminder to resist the temptation of external success and focus instead on spiritual growth and renewal. The invitation to dine with Christ offers a chance for deep, ongoing fellowship, restoring a church from lukewarm faith to a vibrant, faithful community.

The message to Laodicea is timeless. Churches and believers today must guard against spiritual lukewarmness, prioritizing humility, zeal, and a close relationship with Christ over material success. By heeding Christ's call to repent and open the door to His fellowship, the church can move from complacency to vibrant faith, ensuring they remain true to their spiritual calling.

Application for Today—Avoiding the Trap of Spiritual Complacency

The message to the church at Laodicea resonates deeply with many modern churches. It reveals the dangers of spiritual complacency and self-reliance on material wealth over spiritual vitality. Jesus' strong words to Laodicea are a sobering call for churches and individual believers to examine their spiritual condition, repent, and seek true, lasting riches from Him. Through this application, we will delve into the biblical implications of this message, drawing from relevant scriptures and commentary to help believers and churches avoid Laodicea's pitfalls.

1. The Warning Against Spiritual Complacency

Revelation 3:15-16 says, "I know your deeds, that you are neither cold nor hot. I wish you were either one or the other! So, because you are lukewarm—neither hot nor cold—I am about to spit you out of my mouth." Here, Jesus uses the term "lukewarm" (Greek: chliaros, Strong's G5513) to signify spiritual indifference or apathy.

Bible Verse Insight and Commentary

This idea of lukewarmness reflects a state of neither passion nor outright rejection, a dangerous place of spiritual ambivalence. In John 15:5-6, Jesus speaks about the importance of remaining in Him, warning that those who do not are "like a branch that is thrown away and withers." Here, we see that remaining connected to Jesus is essential for spiritual vibrancy. Without a passionate pursuit of Christ, churches and individuals risk becoming "lukewarm" and ineffective.

Practical Application

Today's church must constantly assess its spiritual fervor and avoid complacency. Many churches may start with zeal, but over time, self-sufficiency and routine can dull their fervor. The warning against complacency is a reminder to stay spiritually "hot," continually nurturing a vibrant and personal relationship with Christ, which fuels true spiritual vitality.

2. Rejecting Material Wealth as a Measure of Success

Revelation 3:17 highlights Laodicea's misplaced confidence in its material prosperity: "Because you say, 'I am rich, have become wealthy, and have need of nothing'—and do not know that you are wretched, miserable, poor, blind, and naked." The term "rich" (Greek: plousios, Strong's G4145) refers to worldly wealth, which Laodicea mistook for spiritual blessing.

Bible Verse Insight and Commentary

Material wealth is often seen as a sign of God's blessing, but in the Bible, it can also serve as a distraction. Jesus warns in Matthew 6:19-21, "Do not store up for yourselves treasures on earth, where moths and vermin destroy, and where thieves break in and steal. But store up for yourselves treasures in heaven…" This passage echoes the call to focus on eternal riches rather than temporal wealth. True wealth lies in a life grounded in faith, love, and obedience to Christ.

Practical Application

Churches and believers must be cautious not to equate material wealth or outward success with God's approval. Instead, they should seek a richness in Christ that surpasses all earthly gains. Churches can promote this perspective by encouraging spiritual disciplines, deep prayer lives, and dependence on God's provision, even when resources are plentiful.

3. Pursuing True Riches from Christ

In Revelation 3:18, Jesus counsels the Laodiceans, saying, "I counsel you to buy from Me gold refined in the fire, that you may be rich; and white garments, that you may be clothed." The "gold refined in the fire" (Greek: chrusion pepyromenon ek pyros, Strong's G5557 and G4442) symbolizes a purified faith that is tested and proven.

Bible Verse Insight and Commentary

James 1:2-4 speaks of trials as a refining process, producing perseverance and maturity in faith. Similarly, 1 Peter 1:7 states, "These [trials] have come so that the proven genuineness of your faith—of greater worth than gold… may result in praise, glory, and honor when Jesus Christ is revealed." Spiritual riches are not acquired by wealth but through perseverance, obedience, and a life refined by God's transformative work.

Practical Application

Churches today should emphasize the pursuit of "gold refined by fire," valuing faith and perseverance over material or social status. This could involve encouraging members to view hardships as opportunities for growth, anchoring their faith in God rather than worldly security, and nurturing a heart of humility and purity before God.

4. The Call to Repent and Embrace True Spiritual Life

Revelation 3:19 reminds believers, "As many as I love, I rebuke and chasten. Therefore, be zealous and repent." The term "repent" (Greek: metanoeo, Strong's G3340) signifies a complete turning away from sin and self-sufficiency to genuine faith and dependence on God.

Bible Verse Insight and Commentary

This call to repentance aligns with Acts 3:19, which says, "Repent therefore, and turn back, that your sins may be blotted out." Here, repentance is not just about turning from sin but is an invitation to restoration and fellowship with God. Jesus' rebuke is a form of loving correction, a sign of His commitment to the spiritual welfare of His people.

Practical Application

For churches and believers, repentance should be a continual practice. Recognizing areas of spiritual complacency or self-reliance allows believers to realign with God's purpose and seek renewal. Regular self-examination and an openness to God's correction can restore spiritual vitality and keep believers from drifting into a lukewarm faith.

5. Renewing Fellowship with Christ

In Revelation 3:20, Jesus extends a personal invitation: "Behold, I stand at the door and knock. If anyone hears My voice and opens the door, I will come in to him and dine with him, and he with Me." This image of "knocking" and "opening the door" signifies Christ's desire for intimacy with each believer.

Bible Verse Insight and Commentary

This invitation reflects God's desire for communion with humanity. John 14:23 says, "If anyone loves Me, he will keep My word; and My Father will love him, and We will come to him and make Our home with him." The promise of fellowship with God is at the heart of salvation—an invitation for believers to experience His love, guidance, and presence daily.

Practical Application

The church today must prioritize fostering a close, personal relationship with Christ. This includes regular worship, prayer, and the Word, allowing Him to "dine" with them. This relationship transforms individuals and the church as a whole, filling them with spiritual vitality and keeping them from becoming spiritually "lukewarm."

6. Promise to the Overcomer

In Revelation 3:21, Jesus promises, "To him who overcomes I will grant to sit with Me on My throne, as I also overcame and sat down with My Father on His throne." The term "overcome" (Greek: nikao, Strong's G3528) refers to prevailing through faith and endurance.

Bible Verse Insight and Commentary

This promise of victory resonates with 1 John 5:4-5, which declares, "For everyone born of God overcomes the world. This is the victory that has overcome the world, even our faith." The reward of overcoming is not just earthly blessings but an eternal place with Christ, sharing in His victory and authority.

Practical Application

Believers are encouraged to hold fast to their faith, enduring trials with the hope of eternal reward. Churches can inspire members by highlighting the eternal perspective— reminding them that this life is temporary, but their faithfulness will be richly rewarded in the kingdom of God.

The message to the church at Laodicea is a timely warning and encouragement for churches and believers today. It challenges them to move beyond outward success and self-sufficiency and to pursue a vibrant, passionate faith marked by purity, humility, and genuine dependence on Christ. By heeding this message, churches can avoid the trap of spiritual complacency and remain "hot" in their devotion, continually seeking Christ and bearing the spiritual fruit that pleases Him.

CHAPTER 08

THE PROPHETIC NATURE OF THE SEVEN CHURCHES

Introduction to the Prophetic Layers of the Seven Churches

The seven churches addressed in Revelation (Ephesus, Smyrna, Pergamum, Thyatira, Sardis, Philadelphia, and Laodicea) provide valuable insight into various aspects of Christian life and spiritual conditions. However, they also carry a prophetic significance, representing distinct periods in church history that span from the apostolic age to the present day. In this chapter, we will examine the prophetic interpretations of each church, demonstrating how each represents a historical era and also speaks to conditions still present in the global church today.

1. Ephesus: The Apostolic Church (30–100 AD)

Scripture Reference: Revelation 2:1-7

The church of Ephesus is seen as representing the apostolic church, which had a fervent love for Christ but struggled to maintain its initial passion.

Historical Background

The early church was characterized by strong doctrinal purity and zeal. However, by the end of the first century, some believers began to lose their "first love." Revelation 2:4 states, "Nevertheless, I have this against you, that you have left your first love." The phrase "left your first love" (Greek: agapen sou ten proten, Strong's G26) suggests a gradual shift from initial devotion and passion.

Prophetic Meaning

Ephesus represents the apostolic period, a time of foundational teaching, evangelism, and purity. As the early church faced challenges and persecutions, it began to prioritize structure and organization over fervent personal devotion to Christ, a pattern seen in churches today that focus on orthodoxy but sometimes lack passion.

Application for Today

The lesson of Ephesus is a call for today's church to rekindle its first love for Christ, prioritizing relational devotion alongside doctrinal truth.

2. Smyrna: The Persecuted Church (100–313 AD)

Scripture Reference: Revelation 2:8-11

Smyrna is the church that endured persecution, reflecting the period when Christianity was an outlawed faith in the Roman Empire.

Historical Background

This period saw waves of persecution under emperors like Nero and Diocletian. Revelation 2:10 says, "Do not fear any of those things which you are about to suffer… be faithful until death, and I will give you the crown of life." The "crown of life" (Greek: stephanos tes zoes, Strong's G4735 and G2222) represents eternal life, a promise to those who withstand trials.

Prophetic Meaning

Smyrna symbolizes the persecuted church era, where Christians faced martyrdom and hardship yet remained steadfast. This period refined the church's faith, with many dying for their belief in Christ.

Application for Today

The church today faces persecution in various parts of the world, and Smyrna's example reminds believers to remain faithful even under extreme trials, knowing that God rewards those who endure.

3. Pergamum: The Compromised Church (313–600 AD)

Scripture Reference: Revelation 2:12-17

Pergamum represents a period when the church, having gained acceptance in society, began compromising with pagan practices.

Historical Background

Constantine's Edict of Milan (313 AD) legalized Christianity, bringing it out of persecution but also leading to compromise as pagan influences entered the church. Revelation 2:14 mentions "the doctrine of Balaam," a symbol of compromising truth with idolatry and immorality (Greek: didache Balaam, Strong's G1322).

Prophetic Meaning

The church of Pergamum reflects the compromise of truth with worldly power, blending Christian worship with pagan practices. This period marked a shift where the church began aligning with political authority, diluting its purity.

Application for Today

Pergamum's message cautions modern churches against compromising biblical truths to gain acceptance or power. It is a call to resist blending Christian faith with worldly values.

4. Thyatira: The Corrupt Church (600–1517 AD)

Scripture Reference: Revelation 2:18-29

The church of Thyatira represents the Middle Ages, a period marked by moral and doctrinal corruption within the church.

Historical Background

This era saw the rise of influential figures who led the church into practices and beliefs diverging from scriptural teachings, including indulgences and idolatry. Revelation 2:20 condemns the church for tolerating "that woman Jezebel" (Greek: Iezabel, Strong's G2403), symbolizing false teaching and moral corruption.

Prophetic Meaning

Thyatira represents the medieval church, a time when false teachings and corrupt practices became prevalent. This corruption reflects the church's tolerance of practices that deviated from biblical instruction.

Application for Today

Thyatira's lesson is a reminder of the importance of doctrinal purity and ethical integrity within the church. Churches must uphold biblical teachings and avoid tolerating moral or theological corruption.

5. Sardis: The Dead Church (1517–1750 AD)

Scripture Reference: Revelation 3:1-6

Sardis represents a period when the church had a reputation for being alive but was spiritually dead.

Historical Background

This period corresponds to the Protestant Reformation, where there was a movement away from the corrupted church. Yet, despite reformation, many churches still experienced spiritual stagnation. Revelation 3:1 says, "I know your works, that you have a name that you are alive, but you are dead." The word "dead" (Greek: nekros, Strong's G3498) symbolizes spiritual lifelessness.

Prophetic Meaning

Sardis reflects a reformation period that sought revival but often failed to achieve lasting spiritual renewal, revealing a focus on reputation over real vitality.

Application for Today

Sardis encourages believers to seek genuine spiritual renewal, examining whether their faith is vibrant or merely a facade.

6. Philadelphia: The Faithful Church (1750–1900 AD)

Scripture Reference: Revelation 3:7-13

Philadelphia represents a period of missionary expansion and revival.

Historical Background

The Great Awakenings and missionary movements emerged during this time, with believers zealously spreading the gospel worldwide. Revelation 3:8 says, "See, I have set before you an open door, and no one can shut it." The "open door" (Greek: thyra anoigo, Strong's G2374) symbolizes opportunities for evangelism and spiritual growth.

Prophetic Meaning

Philadelphia represents a period of global evangelism, characterized by faithfulness and dedication to Christ's commission.

Application for Today

Philadelphia's example urges the church to continue in missionary work and evangelism, remaining faithful to Christ despite obstacles, knowing that He provides open doors for ministry.

7. Laodicea: The Lukewarm Church (1900 AD–Present)

Scripture Reference: Revelation 3:14-22

Laodicea is commonly interpreted as representing the modern church, marked by material wealth but spiritual complacency.

Historical Background

Revelation 3:16 describes Laodicea as "lukewarm" (Greek: chliaros, Strong's G5513), indicating spiritual apathy and self-reliance rather than dependence on Christ. This era saw the rise of prosperity and self-sufficiency, causing many churches to value material wealth over spiritual depth.

Prophetic Meaning

Laodicea represents the contemporary church, struggling with spiritual fervor while often prioritizing comfort and material success.

Application for Today

The Laodicean message calls for repentance and a return to spiritual fervor, reminding churches to seek genuine faith and reliance on Christ rather than worldly security.

The prophetic messages to the seven churches serve as a powerful reminder of the spiritual conditions that have recurred throughout church history. Each church represents not only a historical era but also enduring challenges and lessons relevant to today's global church. The call to "hear what the Spirit says to the churches" (Revelation 3:22) emphasizes the need for discernment and faithfulness as the church navigates the complexities of the modern world, preparing for Christ's return and seeking to be a faithful witness in every generation.

CHAPTER 09

THE RELATIONSHIP BETWEEN WORKS AND FAITH IN THE SEVEN CHURCHES

Works as Evidence of Faith

In the letters to the seven churches in Revelation (chapters 2 and 3), Jesus repeatedly highlights their works, using these as markers of their spiritual condition. This focus on works reveals a critical theme: while works do not earn salvation, they are evidence of genuine faith. As James 2:14-26 emphasizes, "faith without works is dead." Jesus' words to each church echo this principle, as He commends or rebukes them based on the nature of their deeds, encouraging self-reflection and repentance.

Purpose of This Study

This chapter will provide a verse-by-verse analysis with strong concordance references and a theological examination of how works manifest faith. We will explore how each church's works reflect their faith and spiritual health, reinforcing the biblical truth that authentic faith is inherently active and outwardly visible.

Works and Faith: A Scriptural Foundation

The Bible consistently presents works as evidence of faith rather than its source. Ephesians 2:8-10 clarifies that believers are saved by grace through faith, but they are created in Christ "for good works, which God prepared beforehand." This foundational understanding is crucial when studying the seven churches.

Verse-by-Verse Analysis and Commentary with Strong Concordance

Revelation 2:2 - The Works of Ephesus: Persistent but Missing Passion

> "I know thy works, and thy labour, and thy patience, and how thou canst not bear them which are evil."

Strong's Concordance Analysis

- Works (Greek: ergon, Strong's G2041): Actions, deeds, or tasks done in service, particularly those driven by faith.

Commentary

Ephesus was commended for its diligent works, patience, and commitment to discern truth from falsehood. However, despite these praiseworthy deeds, they were rebuked for losing their first love (Revelation 2:4). This example reveals that while works are essential, they must be motivated by genuine love for Christ to have spiritual value. For today's church, this warns against empty activity and encourages a renewal of heartfelt devotion as the basis for action.

Revelation 2:19 - The Works of Thyatira: Commendable Yet Compromised

> "I know thy works, and charity, and service, and faith, and thy patience, and thy works; and the last to be more than the first."

Strong's Concordance Analysis

- Charity (Greek: agape, Strong's G26): Refers to selfless love, an outworking of faith in tangible care and service to others.

- Service (Greek: diakonia, Strong's G1248): Acts of assistance, service, often involving sacrifice and effort.

Commentary

Thyatira was praised for its increasing deeds of love, service, and faith. However, they tolerated the false prophetess Jezebel, whose teachings led some to sin (Revelation 2:20). The commendable works were overshadowed by spiritual compromise. This teaches that genuine faith produces works of love and service, but such works must be safeguarded by vigilance against compromise. Works rooted in sound doctrine reflect faith accurately, reinforcing the importance of truth in motivating deeds.

Revelation 3:1-2 - The Works of Sardis: The Reputation of Life with Spiritual Death

> "I know thy works, that thou hast a name that thou livest, and art dead. Be watchful, and strengthen the things which remain, that are ready to die."

Strong's Concordance Analysis

- Dead (Greek: nekros, Strong's G3498): Lacking in spiritual life or vitality, implying a separation from the Spirit's work.

Commentary

Sardis presents a cautionary message about the difference between reputation and reality. Though they had the outward appearance of life through their works, they were spiritually dead. This highlights that works alone cannot sustain spiritual life without the indwelling of genuine faith and a vital connection to Christ. For today's believers, this warns against superficial religious activity and calls for a return to authentic faith that produces life-giving deeds.

Theological Insights: Works as the Evidence, Not Source, of Faith

James 2:14-26 - The Complementary Nature of Works and Faith

In James 2:17, James asserts, "faith by itself, if it does not have works, is dead." This statement reflects the truth echoed in Revelation. Faith is not merely intellectual assent but must be accompanied by action, a tangible expression of belief. Faith that does not result in works is incomplete and ineffective.

Key Concepts from James

1. Faith Acts: Faith without works is akin to an empty profession; it remains sterile and unproductive.

2. Works as Validation: Works serve as the evidence that faith is alive, proving the presence of Christ's transformative power.

Prophetic Significance: The Role of Works in the Seven Churches and Today's Church

The works in each of the seven churches are symbolic of the various stages and conditions the church may experience throughout history and in contemporary times. Each church faced unique challenges, from spiritual complacency to false teachings and persecution. Their works, whether commendable or condemnable, served as indicators of their spiritual vitality and readiness for Christ's return.

Revelation 3:8 - Philadelphia's Faithful Works and the Open Door

> "I know thy works: behold, I have set before thee an open door, and no man can shut it: for thou hast a little strength, and hast kept my word, and hast not denied my name."

Strong's Concordance Analysis

- Kept my word (Greek: tereo logos mou, Strong's G5083 & G3056): Holding firmly to the truth of the gospel, demonstrating faithfulness through action.

Commentary

Philadelphia's works were characterized by faithfulness and resilience, even with limited strength. This "open door" represents an opportunity for faithful witness and service. For today's church, it reminds believers to remain steadfast, using whatever influence they have to advance the gospel. Genuine faith embraces opportunities to serve God and maintain commitment, regardless of opposition or personal limitations.

Balancing Works and Faith in a Believer's Life

The letters to the seven churches provide a rich framework for understanding the relationship between works and faith. They affirm that while salvation is a free gift of grace, genuine faith is transformative, resulting in works that align with God's will and purpose. Just as a tree is known by its fruit (Matthew 7:17-20), faith is recognized by its actions. Each church's condition, whether one of commendation or rebuke, offers valuable lessons for how believers today can evaluate and refine their faith through works that honor God and advance His kingdom.

Application for Today

1. Self-Examination: Regularly assess whether your works reflect a living, active faith rooted in a deep love for Christ.

2. Guarding Against Complacency: Like Sardis, beware of merely outward appearances of faith. Genuine faith engages both heart and action.

3. Embracing Opportunities: Like Philadelphia, look for "open doors" to share your faith through service, regardless of personal limitations.

4. Rejecting Compromise: Like Thyatira, maintain the integrity of faith by aligning works with biblical truth, avoiding doctrines that lead to spiritual compromise.

Final Reflection

In Revelation, the seven churches serve as a powerful mirror for the church today. Their deeds reveal the health of their faith, underscoring that works, while not a means to salvation, are vital as evidence of a living, vibrant faith. The letters to these churches are not merely historical accounts but timeless instructions for believers to cultivate a faith that produces works pleasing to God, yielding eternal rewards.

Balancing Faith and Works

The Interdependence of Faith and Works

In Revelation's letters to the seven churches, Christ evaluates each church not solely based on doctrine but on how their beliefs translated into tangible actions. This balance between faith and works underscores the call for obedience and service as expressions of true faith. The message is clear: faith and works must coexist in the Christian life, as works serve as evidence of living faith. This balance, echoed throughout Scripture, encourages believers to pursue both sound doctrine and righteous action, demonstrating the transformative impact of genuine faith.

Scriptural Basis for Faith and Works

The connection between faith and works is a prominent theme in the New Testament. James 2:14-26 is explicit in saying that "faith without works is dead," emphasizing that true faith is not passive but actively engaged in actions reflecting God's will. Ephesians 2:8-10 also clarifies that while salvation is by grace through faith, believers are "created in Christ Jesus for good works."

Verse-by-Verse Analysis and Commentary with Strong's Concordance

Revelation 2:2 - Ephesus: The Works of Perseverance

> "I know thy works, and thy labour, and thy patience, and how thou canst not bear them which are evil…"

Strong's Concordance Analysis

- Works (Greek: ergon, Strong's G2041): Refers to deeds or actions, often emphasizing labor done in service or dedication to God.

- Labour (Greek: kopos, Strong's G2873): Signifies toiling or hard work, particularly that which requires significant effort and endurance.

Commentary

Ephesus was recognized for its labor and patience, traits associated with its commitment to maintaining doctrinal purity and resisting false teachings. However, their works, while commendable, lacked the love that once fueled their faith (Revelation 2:4). This teaches that even steadfast labor and doctrinal vigilance are insufficient without love as the foundation. Faith, expressed through works, must always flow from a genuine love for Christ.

Revelation 2:19 - Thyatira: Increasing Works and Faith

> "I know thy works, and charity, and service, and faith, and thy patience…"

Strong's Concordance Analysis

- Charity (Greek: agape, Strong's G26): Represents selfless, God-centered love, which is the essence of true faith.

- Service (Greek: diakonia, Strong's G1248): Refers to acts of ministry or assistance, often seen as an outflow of faith and love in action.

Commentary

Thyatira was noted for its growing works, love, and faith. However, the church compromised by tolerating the false prophetess Jezebel, which led some believers into sin (Revelation 2:20). This highlights the importance of discerning true doctrine, as works of faith should be rooted in truth and purity. Today's believers must uphold works driven by love and service, paired with discernment to prevent compromise.

Revelation 3:1 - Sardis: A Reputation for Life, but Spiritually Dead

> "I know thy works, that thou hast a name that thou livest, and art dead."

Strong's Concordance Analysis

- Dead (Greek: nekros, Strong's G3498): Symbolizes spiritual lifelessness, often indicating a lack of genuine connection with the Spirit.

Commentary

Sardis had a reputation for being active and "alive," but Jesus declared them spiritually dead. This serves as a sobering reminder that appearance alone does not equate to spiritual health. Genuine faith produces vibrant, Spirit-filled works, while faith devoid of a relationship with Christ leads to spiritual stagnation. Sardis is a call for today's church to evaluate whether works reflect genuine faith or mere appearances.

Revelation 3:8 - Philadelphia: Faithful Works with Limited Strength

> "I know thy works: behold, I have set before thee an open door, and no man can shut it…"

Strong's Concordance Analysis

- Open door (Greek: thura anoigo, Strong's G2374 & G455): Symbolizes opportunities for ministry or spiritual advancement, accessible through faith and God's favor.

Commentary

Philadelphia's works, though accomplished with limited strength, were commended for their faithfulness. This church exemplifies how even modest works, when done in faith, are significant in God's eyes. For believers today, Philadelphia's example underscores that works done in sincere faith, regardless of scale, are fruitful and valued by God.

Exploring the Relationship Between Faith and Works in James 2

James 2:17 - Faith Without Works is Dead

> "Even so faith, if it hath not works, is dead, being alone."

Strong's Concordance Analysis

- Faith (Greek: pistis, Strong's G4102): Refers to trust, belief, and reliance upon God, often evidenced by one's actions.

- Dead (Greek: nekros, Strong's G3498): In this context, it suggests spiritual uselessness or ineffectiveness.

Commentary

James teaches that faith is proven by works, as genuine belief manifests in actions that honor God and reflect His character. Works are the visible evidence of an inward transformation. This principle is evident in Jesus' evaluation of the seven churches, where works—or lack thereof—are a direct reflection of each church's spiritual condition.

Theological Reflections: Works as Evidence, Not the Source, of Salvation

The New Testament consistently affirms that believers are saved by grace through faith. Romans 3:28 declares that one is justified by faith apart from works, yet Ephesians 2:10 follows by stating believers are created for good works. Works, then, are not the root of salvation but its fruit, showing the life of faith in action.

Implications for Today's Believer

1. Active Faith: Like the churches of Revelation, modern believers must see works as an extension of living faith, not as a replacement for it.

2. Examine Motives: As demonstrated in Ephesus, works without love lose spiritual value. Believers must ensure that love and devotion drive their actions.

3. Discernment: Works of faith require alignment with God's truth, as seen in Thyatira's warning against false teaching.

4. Revival of Purpose: For those with a reputation of faith but lacking spiritual vitality, Sardis' example serves as a call to seek genuine, Spirit-led revival.

Prophetic Significance of Faith and Works in the Churches of Revelation

The balance of faith and works in the seven churches symbolizes the journey of the global church throughout history, from vibrant beginnings to seasons of compromise, and finally to a call for faithful perseverance. This prophetic view encourages the church to remain vigilant in both belief and action as the return of Christ draws nearer.

1. Ephesus - Urges the restoration of love as the motivation behind works.

2. Sardis - Calls for authenticity, warning against superficial faith.

3. Philadelphia - Encourages small, faithful acts done in genuine faith.

Faith and Works in the Christian Life

The relationship between faith and works is foundational to Christian living. Jesus' messages to the seven churches reveal that a life of faith is naturally demonstrated through works that reflect God's love and truth. Believers are called to avoid complacency and spiritual stagnation, engaging in works that stem from a deep, transformative relationship with Christ. As the church anticipates Christ's return, may it be vigilant in living out faith through actions that glorify God, demonstrate love, and bear witness to the truth.

Reflection Questions

1. Are your works motivated by love and genuine faith?

2. How does your life reflect the relationship between belief and action?

3. In what ways can you ensure your actions align with the truth of God's Word?

This chapter concludes that faith, when genuine, is never idle. Rather, it actively expresses itself through love, service, and steadfastness in truth. The balance between faith and works, exemplified by the seven churches, remains essential to the spiritual health of believers today.

CHAPTER 10

THE MESSAGE OF THE SEVEN CHURCHES FOR TODAY'S CHURCH

Spiritual Lessons for the Modern Church

The messages to the seven churches in Revelation 2-3 provide timeless insights into the nature of faith, worship, and spiritual life. These seven churches—Ephesus, Smyrna, Pergamum, Thyatira, Sardis, Philadelphia, and Laodicea—each received a unique message tailored to their strengths, weaknesses, and challenges. For modern believers, these churches offer a blueprint of common spiritual conditions and the ways God calls His people to remain faithful. This chapter will explore the lessons each church imparts, drawing parallels to the contemporary Christian experience.

Spiritual Lessons for Today's Church

Each of the seven churches provides distinct spiritual lessons relevant to today's church, illustrating both what God desires and what He warns against in the life of His followers.

Ephesus: The Call to Rekindle First Love (Revelation 2:1-7)

Condition of the Church

Ephesus was known for its labor, patience, and ability to discern false teaching. However, Christ rebuked them for losing their "first love," calling them to return to the love and passion they once held for Him.

Key Lesson

Modern churches can relate to Ephesus' focus on doctrinal purity while sometimes neglecting the essential relationship with Christ. When a church becomes driven by duty rather than devotion, it risks becoming spiritually cold and distant from God.

Strong's Concordance Analysis

- First love (Greek: protos agape, Strong's G4413 & G26): Refers to the initial, passionate love and dedication believers had for Christ, which often wanes over time due to complacency.

Application for Today

This message serves as a reminder to rekindle our love for Christ, allowing it to inspire our service and drive our doctrinal beliefs. Churches today are called to guard against a mechanical approach to faith, rekindling passion for God that fuels all aspects of ministry.

Smyrna: Faithful Endurance Under Persecution (Revelation 2:8-11)

Condition of the Church

Smyrna was known for its poverty and persecution, yet it remained rich in faith. Jesus did not rebuke them but instead encouraged them to endure suffering, promising the "crown of life" to those who remained faithful.

Key Lesson

The message to Smyrna is relevant for believers facing hardship and opposition for their faith. Jesus' encouragement to "fear none of those things" provides hope and courage for the church today, especially in regions where persecution is severe.

Strong's Concordance Analysis

- Crown of life (Greek: stephanos zoe, Strong's G4735 & G2222): Refers to the eternal reward given to those who faithfully endure trials and tribulations, symbolizing victory and eternal life.

Application for Today

Smyrna's example is a call to stay steadfast in the face of suffering, recognizing that earthly hardships are temporary compared to the eternal rewards promised by Christ.

Pergamum: Standing Firm Against Compromise (Revelation 2:12-17)

Condition of the Church

Pergamum held firm to Jesus' name despite being surrounded by pagan practices, yet some in the church followed the teachings of Balaam, leading to moral and spiritual compromise.

Key Lesson

Pergamum warns of the dangers of compromising with worldly beliefs and practices. Today, churches face similar temptations to blend biblical truth with secular ideologies, risking moral and spiritual integrity.

Strong's Concordance Analysis

- Compromise (Greek: synkrino, though not directly referenced, reflects the combining or blending of different beliefs): In Pergamum, it manifested through the influence of Balaam's teachings, which encouraged idolatry and immorality.

Application for Today

Believers today are called to stand firm in truth and avoid the subtle influence of ideologies that conflict with Scripture, ensuring that their faith remains undiluted by worldly values.

Thyatira: Guarding Against False Teachings (Revelation 2:18-29)

Condition of the Church

Thyatira was praised for its love, service, and faith, yet was rebuked for tolerating the false prophetess Jezebel, who misled the church into idolatry and immorality.

Key Lesson

The warning to Thyatira speaks to the necessity of discerning true from false teachings. The influence of deceptive doctrines can infiltrate the church, often under the guise of progressive ideas or alternative interpretations of Scripture.

Strong's Concordance Analysis

- Prophetess Jezebel (Greek: Iezabel, Strong's G2403): This term symbolizes corrupting influences within the church that lead believers away from sound doctrine and toward sinful practices.

Application for Today

Modern churches are challenged to uphold doctrinal purity, rejecting teachings that promote sin or undermine the authority of Scripture. Leaders and believers alike must stay vigilant against any influence that distorts biblical truth.

Sardis: The Call to Wake Up from Spiritual Deadness (Revelation 3:1-6)

Condition of the Church

Though Sardis had a reputation for being alive, Jesus declared it spiritually dead. The church was characterized by complacency and a lack of genuine spiritual vitality.

Key Lesson

The message to Sardis is a call to wake up, urging churches to pursue true revival. Spiritual life is not a matter of reputation but a genuine connection with Christ and a commitment to living out faith in action.

Strong's Concordance Analysis

- Dead (Greek: nekros, Strong's G3498): Refers to spiritual lifelessness, indicating a state of disconnection from God and lacking active faith.

Application for Today

Churches today must evaluate their spiritual health, ensuring they are actively growing in their relationship with Christ. This message encourages self-examination to determine if faith is alive and bearing fruit, rather than relying on past achievements or reputation.

Philadelphia: Encouragement for Faithfulness (Revelation 3:7-13)

Condition of the Church

Philadelphia received no rebuke but was praised for its faithfulness despite having "little strength." Jesus promised them an open door that no one could shut, symbolizing opportunities for ministry.

Key Lesson

Philadelphia teaches the importance of staying faithful, even when resources are limited. God honors faithfulness and creates opportunities for those who remain steadfast in their commitment to Him.

Strong's Concordance Analysis

- Open door (Greek: thura anoigo, Strong's G2374 & G455): Symbolizes opportunities for ministry and spiritual advancement, which are available to those who remain faithful.

Application for Today

This church's example encourages believers to stay committed in the face of adversity, trusting God to provide and bless their efforts. Churches with limited resources or influence are reminded that God values faithfulness over power or size.

Laodicea: The Danger of Lukewarmness (Revelation 3:14-22)

Condition of the Church

Laodicea was rebuked for being lukewarm, neither hot nor cold. Jesus warned that He would "spit them out," emphasizing the need for passionate commitment rather than complacency.

Key Lesson

Laodicea's lukewarm condition warns against spiritual apathy and self-reliance. Churches today risk becoming lukewarm by prioritizing comfort or material success over genuine spiritual fervor and dependence on God.

Strong's Concordance Analysis

- Lukewarm (Greek: chliaros, Strong's G5513): Represents a state of indifference or lack of commitment, often marked by spiritual complacency.

Application for Today

This message calls believers to examine their commitment and return to a fervent relationship with Christ, recognizing the dangers of comfort and self-sufficiency in the Christian life.

Integrating the Lessons of the Seven Churches

The messages to the seven churches form a comprehensive guide for the modern Christian life. They illustrate the spiritual spectrum within the church, from faithful perseverance to dangerous compromise and apathy. Each church's unique situation offers a valuable lesson, reminding us that:

- Love for Christ must drive our faith (Ephesus).

- Perseverance through trials leads to eternal rewards (Smyrna).

\- Discernment guards us from compromise (Pergamum).

\- Purity and doctrinal fidelity are essential (Thyatira).

\- Revival is needed for spiritual vitality (Sardis).

\- Faithfulness is honored by God (Philadelphia).

\- Commitment and fervency are paramount (Laodicea).

These messages challenge the church today to pursue a faith that is both active and deeply rooted in a relationship with Christ, demonstrating the life-giving power of a faith that works. The timeless nature of these messages underscores the enduring relevance of Christ's call to His people across every age.

Call to Repentance and Renewal

The Urgent Call for Renewal

The messages Jesus delivered to the seven churches in Revelation offer a timeless call for the church to remain vigilant, faithful, and committed to Him. While each church faced unique challenges, a constant theme woven through each message is the need for repentance and renewal. Jesus commended their strengths, exposed their weaknesses, and, above all, called them to return to a vibrant, authentic relationship with Him. Today, the urgency for repentance and renewal remains vital for the spiritual vitality of believers and congregations alike.

The Consistent Call to Repentance in the Seven Churches

Each church in Revelation, despite varying spiritual conditions, was exhorted to self-examine, repent, and grow. Repentance is presented not as a one-time act but as an ongoing process of turning away from spiritual complacency, compromise, or idolatry and turning back to God wholeheartedly.

Repentance for Ephesus: Returning to First Love

Scripture Reference: Revelation 2:5

Ephesus was praised for their diligence in truth and their rejection of false apostles, but their love for Jesus had grown cold. Jesus urged them to "remember therefore from where you have fallen; repent and do the works you did at first."

Key Greek Term

- Repent (Greek: metanoeo, Strong's G3340): Meaning to change one's mind or purpose. Here, it implies returning to their original devotion to Christ.

Application and Reflection

The call to Ephesus resonates with believers and churches today. No amount of doctrinal accuracy or external service can replace genuine love for Christ. For modern believers, it's a call to restore intimacy with God, allowing it to fuel all aspects of spiritual life.

Smyrna: Remaining Faithful Amidst Persecution

Scripture Reference: Revelation 2:10

The message to Smyrna differs as it lacks a rebuke. Jesus encourages them to endure suffering with the assurance of eternal reward. While repentance is not explicitly mentioned, the implication is a call to remain steadfast.

Key Greek Term

- Faithful unto death (Greek: pistos mechri thanatou, Strong's G4103 & G2288): Faithfulness even to the point of death underscores the depth of commitment Jesus expects.

Application and Reflection

Smyrna's message calls believers today to stand firm in their faith, especially in the face of challenges. Repentance, in this context, means renewing one's commitment to persevere, embracing a mindset that values spiritual riches over earthly security.

Pergamum: Rejecting Compromise and Holding to the Truth

Scripture Reference: Revelation 2:16

Pergamum's call to repentance stems from their tolerance of teachings that led to moral and spiritual compromise. Jesus warned them to repent or face His judgment.

Key Greek Term

- Repent (Greek: metanoeo, Strong's G3340): Used here to imply a drastic shift from permitting immoral influences to holding fast to truth without compromise.

Application and Reflection

For churches today, the lesson from Pergamum is clear: repentance involves turning away from the acceptance of worldly influences and reaffirming a commitment to biblical truth. It is a call to reject false teachings that conflict with the gospel and stay rooted in the pure doctrine.

Thyatira: Purging False Teachings and Immorality

Scripture Reference: Revelation 2:21-22

The church at Thyatira tolerated the false prophetess Jezebel, who led some into sin. Jesus called for repentance from immorality and idolatry, warning of severe consequences for those who refused.

Key Greek Term

- Tolerate (Greek: eao, Strong's G1439): In Thyatira's context, this term indicates allowing or permitting false teachings to flourish unchecked within the church.

Application and Reflection

The message to Thyatira speaks powerfully to churches today about the need for doctrinal purity and moral integrity. Repentance here involves actively addressing sin within the church, disciplining leaders, and ensuring a commitment to holiness.

Sardis: Awakening from Spiritual Deadness

Scripture Reference: Revelation 3:3

Sardis had a reputation for being alive but was spiritually dead. Jesus called them to "remember… keep it, and repent." Here, repentance is a wake-up call to move beyond appearance to genuine spiritual life.

Key Greek Term

- Wake up (Greek: gregoreo, Strong's G1127): To watch or be vigilant, implying a need for heightened awareness and readiness in their spiritual life.

Application and Reflection

Sardis challenges modern believers to examine the authenticity of their faith. Repentance here calls for spiritual revival, urging believers to renew their relationship with God and cultivate a faith that's alive and active rather than relying on past reputation or accomplishments.

Philadelphia: Encouragement to Hold Fast

Scripture Reference: Revelation 3:11

Philadelphia, though praised, was encouraged to "hold fast what you have." While no specific rebuke or call to repent is issued, their steadfastness amidst opposition highlights the importance of continued faithfulness.

Key Greek Term

- Hold fast (Greek: krateo, Strong's G2902): To seize or retain, emphasizing the importance of perseverance in faith without wavering.

Application and Reflection

Philadelphia's example is an encouragement for believers to persist in their faith. In the context of repentance, it serves as a reminder that staying faithful requires an ongoing commitment to resist pressures that would lead them away from Christ.

Laodicea: Overcoming Spiritual Lukewarmness

Scripture Reference: Revelation 3:19

Laodicea was neither hot nor cold, which Christ found intolerable. He urged them to be "zealous and repent," calling for renewed spiritual passion.

Key Greek Term

- Lukewarm (Greek: chliaros, Strong's G5513): Indicates a state of indifference, a lack of commitment or enthusiasm.

Application and Reflection

The church at Laodicea represents the danger of complacency. Jesus' call to repentance here is a powerful reminder that God desires passionate commitment. This message speaks to believers today who may find themselves in spiritual indifference, calling them to a renewed zeal for God and His purposes.

Overarching Lessons for Today's Church

The themes of repentance and renewal in these seven messages call the church today to an ever-deepening commitment to Christ and a vigilant pursuit of spiritual purity, love, and authenticity. These churches show that repentance is not merely an admission of wrongdoing but a transformative turning back to God.

Faith in Action

- Faith without works is dead (James 2:14-26): Works serve as evidence of a living faith and are essential in demonstrating the love and commitment a believer has to God.

Vigilance Against Compromise

The messages to Pergamum and Thyatira serve as warnings against allowing false teachings or compromising influences to infiltrate the church. Believers are called to hold fast to biblical truth and live out the gospel without compromising with the values of the world.

Cultivating True Spiritual Life

The call to awaken from spiritual deadness, seen in Sardis, and to avoid lukewarm faith, as in Laodicea, challenges modern believers to move beyond superficiality and seek a deeply rooted, vibrant relationship with God.

Enduring Faithfulness

The commendations given to Smyrna and Philadelphia remind believers that even in the face of hardship and limited strength, God values faithfulness. Believers are called to hold fast, knowing that their perseverance in faith leads to eternal reward.

A Church in Constant Renewal

The message of the seven churches reminds today's church of the continuous journey of faith, requiring repentance, renewal, and unwavering dedication to Christ. Through these messages, believers are encouraged to examine their hearts, reject compromise, and embrace the fullness of life that Christ offers to those who remain faithful. The lessons of these churches invite us to return to our first love, overcome spiritual complacency, and be a radiant testimony of God's love and truth in a world that desperately needs Him.

CONCLUSION

OVERCOMING THROUGH CHRIST

The messages to the seven churches in Revelation are filled with encouragement for those who persevere in faith. Jesus speaks directly to each church, highlighting the need for overcoming challenges and steadfastly holding onto faith. The call to be "overcomers" is a reminder that the Christian journey involves ongoing trials, temptations, and a battle against spiritual complacency. Yet, it is through faithfulness to Christ and reliance on His strength that believers can truly overcome.

Victory Through Faithfulness

The call to "overcome" appears repeatedly in Jesus' messages to the churches (Revelation 2-3), and each time, the promise of reward reinforces the importance of enduring faith. Jesus offers specific blessings to those who conquer through faith in Him:

- The Crown of Life (Revelation 2:10): The church in Smyrna, enduring persecution, is promised the crown of life. This crown symbolizes eternal life and reward for those who endure hardship with faith.

- White Garments (Revelation 3:5): Jesus promises white garments to those in Sardis who overcome. White garments represent purity, victory, and righteousness bestowed upon the believer through Christ.

- Ruling with Christ (Revelation 3:21): The church in Laodicea is invited to sit with Christ on His throne. This reward signifies the ultimate victory and authority that come through faithfulness to Jesus.

Overcoming by Relying on Christ

Overcoming is not achieved by human strength or religious works alone but through reliance on Christ. As John wrote in his first epistle, "For everyone who has been born of God overcomes the world. And this is the victory that has overcome the world—our faith" (1 John 5:4, ESV). Faith in Christ empowers believers to withstand the trials of life, resist the pull of compromise, and rise above spiritual complacency. This victory is available to all who commit themselves to Christ and walk in obedience to His word.

Promises to the Faithful

The promises to the overcomers are not limited to future blessings but also reflect present spiritual realities that believers can experience in their walk with God. In the letters to the seven churches, Jesus promises:

- Protection and Provision (Revelation 3:10): To the church in Philadelphia, Jesus promises to protect them from the "hour of trial." This protection is a symbol of God's provision for His faithful followers, even amidst difficult circumstances.

- A New Name (Revelation 2:17): Those who overcome are given a "new name," signifying a new identity in Christ. This promise reflects the believer's transformation and the assurance of a secure relationship with God.

- The Tree of Life (Revelation 2:7): Jesus promises access to the tree of life for those who overcome, symbolizing the eternal life that is found only in Him.

These promises reinforce the hope and assurance that, while the path may be challenging, the rewards of staying faithful to Jesus far exceed the cost. Each promise Jesus offers is designed to inspire believers toward perseverance and steadfastness in their faith journey.

The Call for Today's Church

The lessons from the seven churches serve as both a warning and an encouragement. They call today's church to remain vigilant, rooted in Scripture, and steadfast in devotion to Christ. As modern believers, we are called to overcome the distractions, compromises, and challenges that threaten our relationship with God. This call is both personal and corporate, urging the church as a whole to continually seek renewal and repentance.

A Final Exhortation

The promise of overcoming is not just for individual believers but for the entire body of Christ. As Jesus said, "To him who overcomes, I will grant to sit with Me on My throne, as I also overcame and sat down with My Father on His throne" (Revelation 3:21, NKJV). This promise invites believers to participate in Christ's victory and reign with Him. Ultimately, the journey of faith is about aligning ourselves with Jesus, the one true Overcomer, and trusting Him to lead us into victory.

Persevering in Christ

The call to overcome through Christ is a call to remain faithful, vigilant, and devoted to God's truth. It is a call to seek renewal, pursue righteousness, and rely on Jesus as our source of strength. The rewards that await those who overcome—eternal life, purity, and authority—are reminders that faithfulness to Christ is not in vain. Believers are called to hold fast to their faith, resisting the temptation to compromise, and keeping their focus on Jesus, who alone provides the strength to endure. Through Him, the victory is already won.

BIBLE STUDY QUESTIONS ON THE SEVEN CHURCHES OF ASIA

The following study questions are designed to help readers reflect on the messages to each of the seven churches in Revelation. These questions can be used individually, in small groups, or in church studies to encourage deeper understanding and personal application of the lessons conveyed to each church.

1. Ephesus — The Church That Lost Its First Love (Revelation 2:1-7)

- What were the commendable qualities of the church in Ephesus, and how do they compare with qualities in your church or personal faith journey?

- Jesus rebuked Ephesus for abandoning its "first love." What do you think this means?

- Reflecting on your own life, is there an area where you have lost your initial passion for Christ? What steps could you take to rekindle this love?

- Why is it significant that Jesus called them to remember and repent? How do these actions contribute to spiritual renewal?

2. Smyrna — The Persecuted Church (Revelation 2:8-11)

- Why do you think Jesus commended the church in Smyrna despite their struggles with poverty and persecution?

- Jesus told them, "Do not be afraid of what you are about to suffer." How does this message of encouragement apply to Christians facing trials today?

- What is the "crown of life" promised to those who are faithful unto death? How does this promise encourage you in your own walk with Christ?

- How does Smyrna's faithfulness in the face of persecution challenge the modern church's response to trials?

3. Pergamum — The Compromising Church (Revelation 2:12-17)

- What was the spiritual climate of Pergamum, and how did it influence the church's actions?

- What does it mean to "hold fast" to Jesus' name in a culture opposed to Christian values?

- The church in Pergamum tolerated false teachings. What are some "doctrines of Balaam" or forms of compromise you see in the church today?

- How can Christians be vigilant against spiritual compromise while remaining compassionate toward others?

4. Thyatira — The Church of False Prophets (Revelation 2:18-29)

- Jesus praised the church in Thyatira for their good works, yet rebuked them for tolerating false teaching. What does this tell us about the importance of doctrinal purity?

- Reflect on how the church in Thyatira was influenced by the "prophetess" Jezebel. How can Christians discern and respond to false teachings today?

- How does tolerance of sin and false teaching affect a congregation's spiritual health?

- What steps can we take to ensure we are growing in both love and truth?

5. Sardis — The Dead Church (Revelation 3:1-6)

- What does it mean for a church to have a "reputation of being alive" but to be spiritually dead?

- Jesus called Sardis to "wake up" and strengthen what remained. How can we apply this message in our own lives?

- What are some signs of spiritual complacency? In what areas might you or your church need a spiritual revival?

- How does the promise of being clothed in "white garments" inspire you to pursue a vibrant, living faith?

6. Philadelphia — The Faithful Church (Revelation 3:7-13)

- Philadelphia is commended for its perseverance. What challenges do you think they faced, and how did they overcome them?

- Jesus promises an "open door" to those who are faithful. What opportunities might God be opening for you or your church as a result of your faithfulness?

- How can we remain strong in faith even when we feel we have "little strength"?

- Reflect on the reward of being made a "pillar in the temple of God." What does this symbolize about stability and security in Christ?

7. Laodicea — The Lukewarm Church (Revelation 3:14-22)

- Why does Jesus describe the Laodicean church as "lukewarm"? What might this look like in a modern context?

- Jesus calls them to "buy from Me gold refined in the fire." How can we pursue spiritual wealth instead of material wealth?

- Reflect on areas in your life where spiritual complacency may be present. What steps can you take to cultivate a passionate, sincere relationship with Christ?

- Jesus invites the Laodiceans to open the door and fellowship with Him. How does this invitation speak to the importance of a personal relationship with Christ?

General Reflection Questions on the Seven Churches

- What do the praises and rebukes of each church reveal about Jesus' expectations for His followers?

- Which of the seven churches do you most identify with personally, and why?

- How can you apply the lessons from each church to strengthen your own faith and relationship with God?

- Consider the "overcomer" promises given to each church. How do these promises encourage you in your journey of faith?

These questions are designed to provoke thoughtful consideration and meaningful discussion, allowing believers to examine their lives and the state of the church in light of Jesus' words to the seven churches. By understanding and applying these messages, we can strive to live as faithful, passionate followers of Christ in today's world.

ENDNOTES AND REFERENCES

The following references provide scriptural, historical, and theological sources to support the analysis and insights offered throughout the study of the seven churches in Revelation. These sources aim to enhance the reader's understanding of biblical themes, church history, and interpretive perspectives.

Scriptural References

- The Holy Bible — Primary source for all scripture references. Recommended translations include:

- New King James Version (NKJV)

- English Standard Version (ESV)

- New International Version (NIV)

- Strong's Exhaustive Concordance of the Bible — James Strong. Provides original Hebrew and Greek terms with contextual meaning and interpretation. Essential for understanding nuanced language in the original texts.

Historical and Theological Commentaries

1. Beale, G. K. The Book of Revelation: A Commentary on the Greek Text. New International Greek Testament Commentary. Grand Rapids: Eerdmans, 1999.

- A comprehensive academic commentary on Revelation, focusing on linguistic and theological analysis.

2. Mounce, Robert H. The Book of Revelation. Revised Edition. New International Commentary on the New Testament. Grand Rapids: Eerdmans, 1998.

- An accessible yet scholarly commentary with in-depth historical context relevant to each church.

3. Keener, Craig S. Revelation. NIV Application Commentary. Grand Rapids: Zondervan, 2000.

- This work emphasizes the practical application of Revelation, blending scholarly insights with contemporary relevance.

4. Wilson, Mark. Biblical Turkey: A Guide to the Jewish and Christian Sites of Asia Minor. Istanbul: Ege Yayınları, 2010.

- Explores the geography, archeology, and history of Asia Minor, providing valuable background on each church's setting.

5. Ramsay, Sir William M. The Letters to the Seven Churches of Asia. London: Hodder & Stoughton, 1904.

- A classic historical examination of the seven churches, focusing on their cultural and sociopolitical settings.

Topical Theological Works

1. Walvoord, John F. The Revelation of Jesus Christ: A Commentary. Chicago: Moody Press, 1966.

- Focuses on prophetic themes in Revelation, offering insight into each church's potential future implications.

2. Swete, Henry Barclay. Commentary on Revelation: The Greek Text with Introduction, Notes, and Indexes. Grand Rapids: Kregel Publications, 1977.

- This commentary offers deep linguistic and textual analysis, focusing on the Greek language's original meaning.

3. MacArthur, John. Because the Time is Near: John MacArthur Explains the Book of Revelation. Chicago: Moody Publishers, 2007.

- Provides a conservative evangelical perspective on Revelation, offering practical and doctrinal insights for today's church.

Historical and Cultural Context

1. Ferguson, Everett. Backgrounds of Early Christianity. 3rd ed. Grand Rapids: Eerdmans, 2003.

- Essential for understanding the cultural, political, and religious context of the early Christian churches.

2. Hemer, Colin J. The Letters to the Seven Churches of Asia in Their Local Setting. Grand Rapids: Eerdmans, 1989.

- An in-depth analysis of the seven churches, focusing on archeological and historical evidence.

3. Witherington, Ben. Revelation. New Cambridge Bible Commentary. Cambridge: Cambridge University Press, 2003.

- Offers a scholarly perspective on the historical context and theological significance of each church.

4. Bauckham, Richard. The Theology of the Book of Revelation. Cambridge: Cambridge University Press, 1993.

- Discusses the overarching theological themes of Revelation, emphasizing God's sovereignty and the call to faithfulness.

Study Bible Resources

1. The ESV Study Bible. Wheaton: Crossway, 2008.

- Includes detailed study notes, maps, and articles relevant to the seven churches.

2. The NKJV Study Bible. Nashville: Thomas Nelson, 2007.

- Provides commentary on key passages and doctrinal insights.

3. The Zondervan NIV Study Bible. Grand Rapids: Zondervan, 2011.

- Known for its historical and theological commentary on each book of the Bible.

Digital Resources

1. Blue Letter Bible (https://www.blueletterbible.org)

- Offers access to Strong's Concordance, interlinear tools, and various translations for deeper study.

2. Bible Hub (https://biblehub.com)

- A helpful resource for accessing multiple commentaries, Greek/Hebrew tools, and maps related to biblical texts.

3. Logos Bible Software

- Provides a comprehensive library of commentaries, linguistic tools, and historical resources for in-depth study.

Endnotes

1. [Endnote on Historical Context for Ephesus] — Information on Ephesus' religious climate drawn from *Biblical Turkey: A Guide to the Jewish and Christian Sites of Asia Minor* by Mark Wilson, pp. 123-130.

2. [Endnote on Doctrine of Balaam in Pergamum] — Insight into false doctrines from The Book of Revelation: A Commentary on the Greek Text by G. K. Beale, pp. 215-220.

3. [Endnote on Jezebel in Thyatira] — Analysis of spiritual compromise in Thyatira drawn from The Revelation of Jesus Christ: A Commentary by John F. Walvoord, pp. 96-98.

This appendix and endnotes section can serve as a foundation for further study and reflection, equipping readers to explore the rich and complex messages given to the seven churches.

COMMON BIBLICAL ABBREVIATIONS

Here's a guide to common abbreviations used in biblical and theological studies, particularly in reference to the text and analysis of Revelation:

Common Biblical Abbreviations

- NKJV - New King James Version (a modern English translation of the Bible)

- ESV - English Standard Version (a more literal translation popular in scholarly and church settings)

- NIV - New International Version (a widely used, thought-for-thought translation)

- KJV - King James Version (the classic English translation from the 17th century)

- BLB - Blue Letter Bible (a digital platform with Bible study tools like concordances and interlinear texts)

Study and Commentary Abbreviations

- Gk. - Greek (language of the New Testament)

- Heb. - Hebrew (language of the Old Testament)

- NIGTC - New International Greek Testament Commentary (a respected academic commentary series focusing on the Greek text)

- NICNT - New International Commentary on the New Testament (a widely used scholarly commentary series)

- NIVAC - NIV Application Commentary (commentaries that focus on applying biblical texts to modern life)

- Eerd. - Eerdmans (a Christian publishing company known for theological and biblical books)

- Int. - Interpretation (commonly used for "Interpretation Commentary" or as shorthand for interpretative study)

Tools and Terms

- Strong's - Refers to Strong's Concordance, a tool indexing every word in the King James Bible and linking it to original Hebrew or Greek words

- Intlin. - Interlinear (a type of Bible that presents original language text alongside translation)

- Logos - Refers to Logos Bible Software, a digital tool for biblical studies with extensive resources for scholarly research

- Exegesis - Critical explanation or interpretation of a text, especially scripture

- Concord. - Concordance (an alphabetical listing of words and phrases in the Bible, showing where they appear)

These abbreviations provide a shorthand for identifying Bible translations, scholarly resources, and terms relevant to theological study, especially for those delving into scripture analysis. Let me know if you'd like more details on any specific abbreviation!

Here's a comprehensive list of Bible verses referenced in the study of the Seven Churches of Asia and their prophetic and practical applications. These verses provide both context and support for the teachings in each chapter, as well as for understanding the balance between faith and works, the call to repentance, and the promise of eternal rewards.

Primary Verses on the Seven Churches

1. Revelation 2:1-7 – Ephesus (The Church that Lost Its First Love)

2. Revelation 2:8-11 – Smyrna (The Persecuted Church)

3. Revelation 2:12-17 – Pergamum (The Compromising Church)

4. Revelation 2:18-29 – Thyatira (The Church of False Prophets)

5. Revelation 3:1-6 – Sardis (The Dead Church)

6. Revelation 3:7-13 — Philadelphia (The Faithful Church)

7. Revelation 3:14-22 — Laodicea (The Lukewarm Church)

Supporting Verses on Works and Faith

1. James 2:14-26 – Faith without works is dead.

2. Matthew 7:21-23 – Only those who do the Father's will enter the kingdom of heaven.

3. Ephesians 2:8-10 – Saved by grace, created for good works.

4. 1 Corinthians 15:58 — Be steadfast, immovable, always abounding in the work of the Lord.

5. Philippians 2:12 – Work out your salvation with fear and trembling.

Verses on Repentance and Renewal

1. 2 Chronicles 7:14 — If my people…will humble themselves and pray and seek my face and turn from their wicked ways.

2. Acts 3:19 – Repent and turn to God, so that your sins may be wiped out.

3. Romans 12:2 – Be transformed by the renewing of your mind.

4. 2 Peter 3:9 — The Lord is patient…not wanting anyone to perish, but everyone to come to repentance.

Verses on Overcoming and Perseverance

1. Revelation 2:10 – Be faithful unto death, and I will give you the crown of life.

2. 1 John 5:4-5 – Everyone born of God overcomes the world.

3. Romans 8:37 – We are more than conquerors through him who loved us.

4. Hebrews 10:23-25 – Hold fast the confession of hope; consider how to stir up one another.

Promises to the Overcomer in Revelation

1. Revelation 2:7 – To him who overcomes, I will give to eat from the tree of life.

2. Revelation 2:11 – He who overcomes shall not be hurt by the second death.

3. Revelation 2:17 – To him who overcomes…I will give him a white stone.

4. Revelation 2:26-28 – To him who overcomes…I will give power over the nations.

5. Revelation 3:5 – He who overcomes shall be clothed in white garments.

6. Revelation 3:12 – To him who overcomes, I will make a pillar in the temple of My God.

7. Revelation 3:21 – To him who overcomes, I will grant to sit with Me on My throne.

Additional Verses for Reflection

1. Matthew 25:14-46 – Parable of the talents; the importance of faithful service.

2. 1 Timothy 4:13-16 – Persist in doctrine and personal growth.

3. Hebrews 4:11 – Let us be diligent to enter God's rest, lest anyone fall through disobedience.

4. Galatians 6:7-10 – Whatever a man sows, that he will also reap.

5. Jude 1:20-21 – Build yourselves up…keep yourselves in God's love.

These verses reflect the lessons and themes from each of the Seven Churches, focusing on the relationship between faith, works, repentance, and the promises given to those who persevere. Let me know if you would like additional commentary on any of these passages!